CONTEMPORARY SOUTHERN HOMES

E. ASHLEY ROONEY

Foreword by Carl Abbott

Schiffer Publishing Ltd
4880 Lower Valley Road • Atglen, PA 19310

Library of Congress Control Number: 2014942991

Photo Credits: Front cover: Guy Peterson. Photo@ Greg Wilson; backcover: Studio WTA. Jeffrey Johnston; inside cover. Carter & Burton. Russell Abraham Photography. Image Flipped. FIX; back flap: Carl Abbott. © Steven Brooke Studios; title page. Glavè & Holmes. Ansel Olson; Contents page: Mark Hampton ©Steven Brooke.

Designed by Brenda McCallum
Cover design by RoS
Type set in Futura

Published by Schiffer Publishing, Ltd.
4880 Lower Valley Road
Atglen, PA 19310
Phone: (610) 593-1777
Fax: (610) 593-2002
E-mail: Info@schifferbooks.com

For our complete selection of fine books on this and related subjects, please visit our website at www.schifferbooks.com. You may also write for a free catalog.

This book may be purchased from the publisher. Please try your bookstore first.

We are always looking for people to write books on new and related subjects. If you have an idea for a book, please contact us at proposals@schifferbooks.com.

Schiffer Publishing's titles are available at special discounts for bulk purchases for sales promotions or premiums. Special editions, including personalized covers, corporate imprints, and excerpts can be created in large quantities for special needs. For more information, contact the publisher.

ISBN: 978-0-7643-4682-8
Printed in China

CONTENTS

Foreword: A Place of Wonder
by Carl Abbott FAIA 5
Introduction 11
Contemporary Architects and Designers 17
- Carl Abbott FAIA 18
- Alterstudio Architecture LLP 28
- The Anderson Studio of Architecture and Design ... 40
- Bercy Chen Studio LP 56
- Marlon Blackwell Architect 72
- Carter+Burton Architecture PLC 84
- Glavè & Holmes Architecture 92
- Guyon Architects Incorporated/ The Studio for Architecture 104
- Mark Hampton, FAIA 114
- Frank Harmon Architect PA 126
- McCollough Architecture, Inc. 138
- Moon Bros. Inc. Architects 150
- Shawn O'Brien Interiors 164
- Guy Peterson | Office of Architecture 178
- L. Craig Roberts 186
- studioWTA 204
- Thomas & Denzinger Architects 222
- Tonic Design | Tonic Construction 244
- Ed Weber Architects 252
- Andrew A. Willett Architect PA 268

Publications and Awards 300
Index 303
Acknowlegments 303

Casa Del Cielo. Photo © Steven Brooke.

FOREWORD

A PLACE OF WONDER

Carl Abbott FAIA

In the U.S. South, the land is among the most beautiful and diverse of any place on Earth. In the lore of the early explorers of the New World, there are many sentiments in awe of the land—so marvelous that it seems a man would never want to leave this earthly paradise... these mountains are most beautiful, slopes filled with trees so tall, they seem to touch the sky.... here there are marvelous big lakes, rivers and harbors beyond compare... the islands are the most beautiful... a place of wonder.

The South is a land with a great range in climate and topography—from the majestic mountains to the lowlands stretching out to the Gulf of Mexico, the vast Atlantic Ocean, and the islands with beaches reaching out to the horizons of infinity.

Look around you. Does your home embrace the beauty of nature? I recall my early years in a small town in coastal Georgia: giant oak trees heavy with Spanish moss, the vast expanses of marsh, a sea of grass with seasonal transformation from brown to green then gold, the rivers, the animals, the breezes, the changing patterns of the sky. The atmosphere was tactile, the mystery of history was always present: all around were the ruins of the Old South.

My first memory of experiencing architecture was in my aunt's large antebellum home (one of the few buildings in our small town that escaped Sherman's fire in his "March to the Sea"). I recall approaching the house with its wide brick stairway leading up to the porch with its long row of columns. A formal front door led to an entry hall with a grand stair to the upper level bedrooms. The large living room was a tall space with triple-hung windows that reached from floor to ceiling, and there was a sequence of separated rooms: the living hall, dining room, kitchen, and bedrooms. Many years later, I realize that my aunt's home required many servants to make it function. The typical antebellum home was very rigid and symmetrical, with style being more important than function.

Today, the world in which we live is very different. Let's stop and consider where we have come from in the history of architecture and construction. In the early 1900s, the world went through vast social changes that evolved through the Industrial Revolution: the positive birth of the middle class, the devastating pollution and destruction of the city, and the development of many new materials including ferro cement, steel to create large spans, and large panels of glass.

At the same time there were other major changes in movement, in technology, in communication: the automobile, the airplane, electricity, radio, the telephone, the camera. With the camera, many felt this would be the end of painting: why paint a portrait or a landscape, when the camera could more perfectly catch the image. As we all know, the camera did not replace painting; instead, it pushed artists to look more deeply, to reach into their imagination, and create amazing new ways in which to see the world—impressionism, cubism, and abstraction.

House of Columns. Photo © Sean Harris.

Hilltop Residence. Photo © Alison Dunlap.

In the same way, the Industrial Revolution pushed architects to reevaluate the art of architecture. Instead of copying past styles, a whole new way of building was opened.

From this evolved two basic schools of architecture: in Europe the International Style of the Bauhaus and in America the Organic Style of Frank Lloyd Wright. To the Bauhaus, everything came from the machine and the buildings expressed that: engineered steel columns and buildings separate from the land. To Wright, everything came from the earth even if touched by the machine, so the buildings expressed that—stone, wood, buildings nestled in the land.

In the South a unique movement melded these two schools. This movement became the Sarasota School of Architecture, which began in the 1940s. This school became widely known for its innovations in building technology and comfort that made the dreams of modern living in the south a functioning reality. The leading architect in this group was Paul Rudolph, who later became head of Yale's School of Architecture. Through the many international students who were influenced by Rudolph at Yale, the concepts of the Sarasota School spread throughout the world.

Lido Bay Residence. Photo © Steven Brooke.

The Sarasota School learned from traditionally southern details while reinventing them and creating a unique architectural language. Some of these include:

- Grills, trellises, and shutters to filter light
- Deep overhangs to shade and cool the building
- Rows of columns to create outdoor rooms without walls
- The veranda, balcony, and courtyard to extend the living space to the outdoors
- Sun orientation for heat in the winter and coolness in the summer
- The dogtrot plan with breezeways and separation of private and public rooms
- Tall rooms, floor to ceiling windows, clerestories to allow natural ventilation
- Raising the house above the ground to escape dampness.

This approach, old lessons combined with new technologies, formed an architectural movement suited to its region. Doors of sliding glass, brise soleils, walls of hinged shutters, and latticed roof umbrellas create a regional language, a lineage from which our contemporary buildings evolve.

Today there is a sense of freedom— an awareness of our new technologies, new possibilities allowing us to move forward. Walls can now be made of glass to strengthen the connection between inside and out. Spaces, once compartmentalized, are now open and fluid to strengthen family bonds. The kitchen, once a separate space off in a corner, can become the heart for family activity and a major part of the home's function.

Of all building types, the home is the one place that can most clearly support the changes, the needs, the functions, the reality of the people for whom it is constructed. The home expresses the personality of the family through its plan, its color, its texture, and its form. Looking, exploring, can lead you into a new awareness of what is beauty, what is of our time, and what is timeless.

Moving through and around a well-designed building can be a rewarding experience—inviting you to explore the full freedom of our four-dimensional world. This movement through space and time is a unique quality of architecture. Not only is architecture the most public of all the arts, architecture must give protection; it must function and exist in the context of the man-made and the natural.

In this book, you will see many modern homes that work beautifully with the land. Does your home allow you to experience nature? Your home strongly affects the physical and psychological world in which you live. The quality of place can enrich your life. The goal is to create protective, functional designs that are supportive and inspiring environments. As Churchill said "...we shape our buildings, thereafter they shape us."

We want lives that are full of the richness of beauty and light—a home that inspires and supports our busy lives and creates a private world within a world. The modern home, informed by the land, can be a place that will enrich the quality of your life.

Seaside Estate. Photo © Steven Brooke.

Carl Abbott is a practicing architect and speaker. *His work has been published internationally in numerous books, journals, and films. For over four decades, Carl's firm, located in Sarasota, Florida, has been one of the most highly awarded in the South. He graduated cum laude from the University of Florida before studying in the Masters program at Yale under Paul Rudolph. Carl is now the leading member of the innovative Sarasota School of Architecture.*

In addition to the South and the Caribbean, he has worked in Hawaii, in New York with I.M. Pei, and in London with Yale classmates Norman Foster and Richard Rogers. The Florida/Caribbean AIA has honored Abbott with many awards including the Medal of Honor for Design and the Outstanding Architectural Firm Award. Nationally, he was elected an American Institute of Architects Fellow.

IN/FORMED by the LAND, the book of Carl Abbott's award-winning architecture, has received international acclaim.

INTRODUCTION

I remember my first trip to my family's ancestral home in Vicksburg, Mississippi. It was one of the few plantation houses that had survived the Siege of Vicksburg, thanks to a quick-witted ancestor who leaned on her daddy's West Point connections. The house had unusually high ceilings in order to increase the volume of air around the room's occupants. These high ceilings allowed larger windows and doors that admitted the breezes and opened on long, shaded galleries. Those galleries weren't just places to sit and rock, but served to keep the rising and setting sun off windows, doors, and walls. Thus, they contributed to the relative coolness of the house. They also served as halls or corridors through which the household occupants could pass from one room to another. In fact, to get upstairs, I had to use an outside staircase.

Like many southern homes, the original kitchen was in a separate building to protect against the possibility of fire. Surrounded by a schoolhouse, outhouse, and other outbuildings, it had been a bustling, self-supporting community before the Civil War. Today, in the twenty-first century, one distant relative lives in it.

America is a land of immigrants, and the immigrants brought with them their memories, their pots and pans, and the building traditions of their native lands. They found the land in America very different from their expectations, however. The colonists in Virginia quickly discovered that the soil in the Chesapeake region was suitable for tobacco cultivation, and by 1620 Virginia's economy was organized around tobacco. The Lord Proprietors of the Carolinas had assumed they would be ruling over a land of rolling green hills and small farms. Instead of meadows, they found a humid, swampy region. They were dismayed until they realized that southern Carolina's marshy lowlands were an ideal place to grow rice.

The early Southern colonists settled not in towns, as they did in New England, but on sizable acreage scattered throughout the countryside. They were often far removed from each other. Consequently, plantations became small towns themselves, with warehouses, shops, schoolhouses, and the owner's residence. Because so many were near tidewater inlets or slow-moving deep rivers, a planter could send his crop off to London from a dock on his front lawn and never go to town. Those great Southern cities (e.g. Charleston, Savannah, Mobile) were primarily commercial ports through which crops could be shipped.

The pressures of climate and access to building materials and labor modified the Southern colonist's building and farming practices to suit the region. In Virginia, houses were often made of brick, because clay was available in the area. Along the North Carolina coast, the porch or piazza played a dominant role, providing a feeling of elegant grandeur. Built of wood or brick, Southern houses generally had a central entry and either a massive central chimney or a pair of chimneys, one at each end of the house. As time went on, Southerners added raised basements and verandas so the residents could enjoy the cooling breezes. By 1780, plantation houses acquired a full second story, center halls, and interior stairs, and the shotgun house appeared. Only one room wide and three or more rooms deep—shotgun houses were built throughout urban areas in the Deep South. Their length provided excellent airflow, while their narrow width increased the number of lots that could be fitted along a street.

The French sold Louisiana in 1803, Spain ceded Florida in 1819, and the Deep South became a part of the United States. This enormous expanse of land from the Chesapeake Bay to the Mississippi River offered enormous opportunities for enterprising farmers to improve their economic status. The traditional pattern of large landholdings, which had developed first in Virginia and the Carolinas and then down the Atlantic coast, expanded into Louisiana, Mississippi, and Alabama, states that were producing large amounts of cotton. By the next decade, Texas and Arkansas had turned to cotton. The plantation owners built a vast aristocratic life; the southern merchants followed. Slaves provided the labor needed to support the agricultural economy.

As the southern economy thrived on exports of cotton, sugar, rice, and indigo, houses grew in size and taste. This development coincided with the Greek revival style of architecture, with its bold, simple lines, its facade columns, and its great first floor rooms. The growth in the scale and size of these plantation homes continued until the beginning of the Civil War, particularly in the Mississippi Valley. It resulted in the large, white, antebellum mansions of the Deep South with their high ceilings, enormous rooms, and lavish trim. Most of these houses retained the galleries, balconies, and raised first floors from before.

The French influence on Southern building practices is unmistakable. It thrives in areas with long, hot, and humid summers in such places as the Carolinas and Louisiana, and in those areas that are subject to major flooding. Whether built of stone, brick, log, or half-timber, a typical galleried French colonial cottage was characterized by its "T-shaped" floor plan with a gallery that

Located on the Mississippi River in the community of Vacherie, Louisiana, Oak Alley Plantation is protected as a National Historic Landmark. The alley or canopied path created by a double row of live oaks about 800 feet long that was planted in the early eighteenth century runs between the house and the Mississippi River. Today, it is listed on the National Register of Historic Places of the United States. Courtesy of Paul E. Doherty.

encircled the arms of the "T" and the main body of the building. A Gulf Coast settler often elevated his house above ground level to allow it to ride out the heavy rain and many floods that accompanied living in the warm, moist climate and to capture the cool air from underneath the house. Before the Civil War, bathrooms or water closets were rarely seen. Instead, there were outside privies, though the privileged might use commode chairs in their rooms. Kitchens were often housed separately to keep their heat away from the main house.

The War Between the States brought devastation to the South. Most young men, livestock, assets, and investments, other than land, were gone along with some of the major cities. Because of the economic stagnation, planters' homes were often abandoned as people fled the region.

The rebuilding took decades. Kenneth Severens points out in *Southern Architecture* that because of the hardships of Reconstruction, southern buildings survived in considerable numbers after the Civil War. As a result, Victorian architecture never swept into the South as it did in the rest of the country. Those Georgian, Federal, and Greek revival cityscapes and homes that survived the war remained. Interestingly, the leading American architect of the period, Henry Hobson Richardson, was born on a Louisiana plantation and educated in New Orleans, Harvard, and Paris. In the 1870s and 1880s, his buildings could be found throughout the country—except in his native region!

During the latter half of the nineteenth century, the rapid spread of the Industrial Revolution and the easy transport offered by the proliferating railroads led to major changes in designing and building American houses throughout the nation. Previously, builders were limited to what could be found nearby, fabricated, and/or lifted into place manually. By the late 1800s, large factories were producing building components, such as doors, windows, and siding, and shipping them across the country. Advanced woodworking machines and tools, and improved building techniques, such as balloon framing, made elaborate and much larger designs possible and more affordable. Significant improvements were made in modern conveniences. The bathroom replaced the outdoor privy in homes of the wealthy, but wasn't common until the twentieth century. These changes took much longer to occur in the ravaged Southern states.

As the century ended, men who had amassed fortunes in the great expansion of the Industrial Revolution looked for ways to spend them. From the late 1800s to 1920, a period often called the Gilded Age, European-trained architects began to design landmark period houses for the American economic elite or the American "aristocracy" of the time. Bankers, heads of industry, and robber barons, they were the ones with the next daring idea, the next new product, and the next great invention that would help transform the country to an industrialized nation of international standing. They included visionaries such as Henry Flagler, who envisioned St. Augustine as a sunny haven for the wealthy in the Gilded Age; George and Edith Vanderbilt, who built the 250-room family home in Asheville, North Carolina; the Duke family; and Walt Disney who turned 47,000 square miles of Central Florida swamp into Disney World. Refrigeration, air conditioning, and overhead fans helped make the South habitable and appealing to Northerners.

Like my family home in Mississippi, many plantations continued to be lived in as ancestral homes, although there may have been little economic rationale for their maintenance. But their very presence preserved the sense of family

The South today has many preserved mansions and just as many beautiful twenty-first century houses that maintain that same sense of ambience. It has changed from the land I knew as a child. People may still ask my husband "who's your family," but Southerners are actively seeking a sense of community. As we drove through the Deep South, we sat in many restaurants where people of different backgrounds sat together, talked together, and greeted us with warmth.

Their design landscape has changed too. Yes, you can still see those Greek revival columns, but you can also see a remarkable range of residences that skillfully reflects their physical and cultural milieus within the twenty-first century. They may have walls of glass and open floor plans, but they also offer charm and authenticity.

As Maryann Thompson said so eloquently in *Contemporary Boston Architects* (Rooney, 2012):

> Today's lifestyles are profoundly different...We desire different kinds of spaces. Our kitchens, home work spaces, relationships to natural light and landscape, our relationships to technology and energy use, even our closets and the way they are manifested say something about the culture in which we live and the values we support. Because the house is so intimately tied to life, its manifestation becomes a mirror of who we are. As we change, the architectural forms and spaces in which we live innovate.

In the following pages are twenty-one Southern design professionals whose architectural styles vary as much as the region. Their award-winning work ranges from the classical symmetry of Georgian Palladian to modernist traditions infused with fascinating flair. Their work features expansive, open floor plans, the seeming disappearance of the boundary between the exterior and the interior, and the use of indigenous materials. The work of these forward-thinking architects and designers helps us to envision new ways of living in the world.

House of Columns. Photo © Sean Harris.

Built in 1833, Oakleigh is now a historic house museum in Mobile, Alabama. It is the of a group of buildings that contain a working-class raised cottage, a former slave quarters, and a modern archives building. Courtesy of D. Peter Lund.

Florida bayou. D. Peter Lund.

THE **ARCHITECTS,** **BUILDERS,** AND **DESIGNERS**

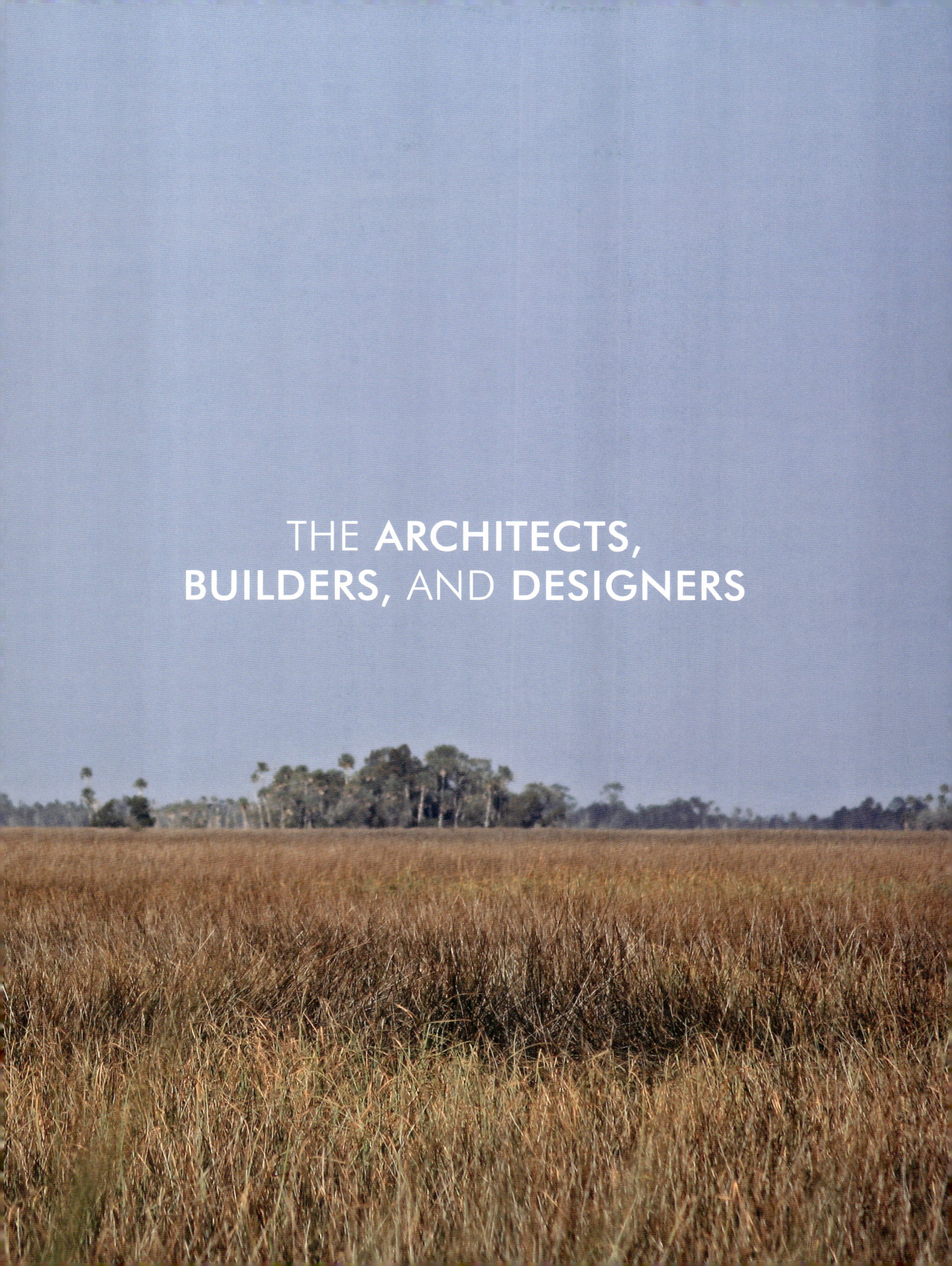

CARL ABBOTT, FAIA

SARASOTA, FLORIDA

Our projects are designed to enrich our client's lives. Each home is in/formed by the land—the breezes, view lines, sounds of the waves, the movement of the sun and stars—natural elements which help define the forms of our buildings.

Florida and the Caribbean are among the most beautiful tropical regions of the earth. Designing for this region is an art/science with lineage to the Sarasota School of Architecture—the world-renowned architectural movement made famous by Paul Rudolph. After studying under Rudolph at Yale, I returned to the South, where I became a part of this important movement, while also developing my own direction.

Wave-like curves, angular forms, and stepped planes enhance the way you experience nature and its ever-changing dance of light. In our architecture, spaces are designed from the intimate to the grand—with unfolding views as you move through and around the home. You become an active participant.

From a palette of natural colors—the silvered trunk of palm, the vibrancy of tropical flora—and materials—sun-bleached wood, natural stone, textured stucco, sea shell, glass—each home is designed to complement the very special sites in which our clients choose to live.

Having worked in large offices internationally, I have kept my firm small to allow for close, personal involvement with each individual. Together, we have created residences, which have won numerous awards; most important, however, are the many acknowledgements from clients who feel their homes have enriched their lives.

Carl Abbott's beautiful spaces are a rare and impressive combination of architectural clarity and humanistic warmth—his architecture has a sense of timelessness.—Lord Norman Foster

2846 Riverside Drive | Sarasota, FL 34234
941-351-5016 | carl@carlabbott.com | www.carlabbott.com

Seaside Estate

This Florida home designed by Carl Abbott opens wide to sweeping views up and down the long stretch of beach. A monumental brise soleil shades the house and terraces from the tropical sun. Photo © Steven Brooke Studios.

The master suite at the highest level—a dramatic sense of floating over the water. Photo © Steven Brooke Studios.

Designed as though the site extended to the horizon, the house is of a grand scale with high ceilings on multiple planes. The shimmer of light on water, the sound of waves, changing breezes, the sense of movement flow into and through the spaces. Photo © Steven Brooke Studios.

A linear pool in the tropical garden leads to the guest house with its rooftop sun terrace and the Gulf beyond. Photo © Steven Brooke Studios.

Casa del Cielo

In the canopy of trees, this silvered-wood house floats on tall concrete columns. Photo © Steven Brooke Studios.

Located on an island in the Gulf of Mexico, this vacation house designed by Carl Abbott is a series of terraces that soar over the land and reach out to a world-famous beach. Photo © Steven Brooke Studios.

Materials that weather well and blend with the environment are used—silvered wood, Mexican tiles, and clear glass. The trees of the site, the beach, the water, and the sky are all perceived as materials of the building. The house is an extension of the site itself. Photo © Steven Brooke Studios.

"The balance of solids and voids and the flow of space horizontally and vertically are handled in a remarkable way."—Paul Rudolph. Photo © Steven Brooke Studios.

Stair detail. Photo © Steven Brooke Studios.

Artist's Waterfront Residence

Screened by a colonnade of royal palms, this Carl Abbott-designed residence on a key off Florida has a monolithic facade with doors leading to a quiet, shell-covered entry court. As with a seashell, there is a solid, protective side and an open side that looks to the sea. Photo © Steven Brooke Studios.

The interior spaces fan out to sweeping views of the Bay. Across the entire water frontage are walls of glass, angled in plan, allowing each room to have different views. The large ceiling planes step upwards, creating an unfolding sequence of spaces. Photo © Steven Brooke Studios.

ALTERSTUDIO ARCHITECTURE LLP

AUSTIN, TEXAS

At Alterstudio, we focus our attention on the relationship between the material facts of architecture and the social occasions it shelters and invites. The work is rooted in deep-seated virtues of architecture—generous space making, shrewd manipulation of day lighting, and meticulous attention to detail. The heightening of direct human experience and the framing of the complex circumstances of their situations are at the core of each project.

Our commitment to enhance and protect both the cultural and natural environments of the communities we serve is evident in the technical craftsmanship of our designs and in the long-term sustainability of our projects. We view the creation of ecologically responsive design as a core value in our office. We promote an ecological approach that acknowledges the impact of finite resources as a positive contributor in the creation of an ethical architecture. It compels, informs, and guides our choices and recommendations during project development strategies, programming, product selection, detailing, specification of materials, and contractor selection. Our approach to sustainable design goes beyond logistical and mechanical elements, to create an architecture that is uplifting to its users and in harmony with its cultural context and natural surroundings.

Widely recognized for our compelling designs and meticulous attention to detail, Alterstudio Architecture has won more than sixty design awards and been regularly published regionally, nationally, and internationally. The office relies on the talent of its three partners and four staff members.

1403 Rio Grande St. | Austin, TX 78701
512-499-8007 | info@alterstudio.net | www.alterstudio.net

Cascadera

A book-matched Carrara marble wall houses a stainless steel fireplace and a vintage hotel mirror to anchor the living room. A bespoke sofa and chairs define a sitting area by the fireplace, while a Lucite table and chairs allow for after dinner bridge. Photo © Paul Bardagjy

Alterstudio's design of the Cascadera residence revolved around the desire for a refined lifestyle, elegant entertaining, and a deep-seated sense of propriety. Photo © Paul Bardagjy.

An uninterrupted corridor stretches the 145-foot length of the building, providing a sense of expanse and continuity throughout the home. Photo © Paul Bardagjy.

The semi-private areas of the house are located in the elbow of the boomerang —a breakfast banquet looking to the north, and a television study for two to the south—connected by a screen of translucent glass and timber. Here, the client is literally caught between two worlds, with one foot in the private and one in the public wings of the house. Photo © Paul Bardagjy.

Abundant light from floor-to-ceiling windows on the south is filtered through elegant sheer curtains and balanced by high clerestory windows across the room. Photo © Paul Bardagjy.

A strong sense of propriety led to a design with clear divisions between public and private, as well as served and service, parts of the home. The roof continues to the street, greeting visitors with a porte cochère and introducing an elegant sequence of spaces on a single level.
Photo © Paul Bardagjy.

Mid-century Modernism and Hollywood Regency décor served as aesthetic touchstones throughout the house. Old molds were found and reused to make the shaped concrete block on the exterior, and vintage lighting and furniture was rejuvenated on the interior.
Photo © Paul Bardagjy.

Hillside

Alterstudio designed a substantial renovation and expansion of a 1927 bungalow. The existing, 1,000 square-foot building was rescued from dilapidation and delineated abstractly in stark white. This was paired with a new, 1,100 square-foot sculptural volume clad in black-stained cypress, connected via a glass entry bridge. Courtesy of Casey Dunn Photography.

Lumber from the existing house was salvaged and repurposed throughout, from shiplap accent walls to counters made from long leaf pine beams to the split-cedar entry steps from the original house piers. Courtesy of Casey Dunn Photography.

Akin to Marcel Breuer's 1943 proposition for a Bi-Nuclear House, Alterstudio split the house into two zones; one for living and socializing, and the other for concentration, work, and sleeping. Courtesy of Casey Dunn Photography.

The addition turns large openings to the back yard, maintaining intimacy while giving the living space a sense of openness. Courtesy of Casey Dunn Photography.

Light wells and skylights are used throughout the home to bring in plenty of natural daylight without sacrificing privacy on the small neighborhood lot. Courtesy of Casey Dunn Photography.

An ultimately modern sensibility in the addition provides a counterpoint to the sense of contained space in the original house. Courtesy of Casey Dunn Photography.

The homeowner worked closely with the architect to select finishes that bring a sense of balance and connection between the different architectural qualities of the existing house and addition. Courtesy of Chad Wadsworth.

Lake View

The visitor arrives by meandering under a grove of ancient trees into an intimate entry sequence of limestone, vertical cypress, and verdant planting. Courtesy of Patrick Y. Wong/ AtelierWong.com.

Alterstudio's unmitigated ceiling plane provides a surface for reflected lighting and creates a sense of continuity while a delicate window wall accentuated by monolithic corner glazing connects the interior to the outdoors. Courtesy of Casey Dunn Photography.

The kitchen is defined by book-matched mahogany cabinetry, huge surfaces of Caesarstone, and a floor-to-ceiling wall of windows. Courtesy of Casey Dunn Photography.

The rich palette of materials and purpose-made cabinetry add a sense of finesse and offer points of stasis to the compelling and omnipresent view. Courtesy of Casey Dunn Photography.

The new house emphasizes view and a dynamic spatial sequence while at the same time creating an abstract backdrop for the serendipity of light, circumstance, and view. Courtesy of Patrick Y. Wong/ AtelierWong.com.

THE ANDERSON STUDIO OF ARCHITECTURE AND DESIGN

CHARLESTON, SOUTH CAROLINA

Like a great relationship, a great house is more than the sum of its parts. Amazing architecture is a marriage of design and structure, art and science, interior and exterior spaces and the experiences they create. The Anderson Studio addresses residential interior design and exterior design as one component. While the studio may formally provide one service or the other, we are constantly designing for both, which makes collaboration with other designers and consultants fluid, very productive, and a genuine asset to our clients.

Through global travels, design studies abroad, and a passion for history, Scott W. Anderson has developed a design philosophy that embraces the close relationship between classicism and modernism; our premise is that the study of great design from the past, combined with innovative creativity, can be used to solve today's complex problems with clear and direct solutions. With more than twenty-two years of architecture experience, our team provides a hands-on approach and the one-on-one attention of a small firm, while offering the expertise, understanding, and capabilities of large architecture firms. Well-known in Charleston as skilled residential architects, our craftsmanship, attention to detail, and ability to translate the visions of our clients have resulted in a long list of repeat clients and a distinctive portfolio of fine residential homes that elevates the business of building to the fine art of architecture.

The Anderson Studio has the skills and training necessary to carry out a wide variety of projects, with the instinct to know what works where. Our team of talented residential architects and interior designers has planned, designed, furnished, and renovated private residential homes, speculative residences, commercial offices, restaurants, historic structures, and luxury resort enclaves. Our designs develop from getting to know our clients' lifestyle, wishes, aesthetic preferences, and the subtleties of each property. Each one of these opportunities allows us the ability to collaboratively create something unique and timeless.

355 Bayview Drive. | Charleston, SC 29464
843-884-0444. | designers@theandersonstudio.com. | www.theandersonstudio.com

The Beach House

This 7,700 square-foot Shingle-style beach house on Kiawah Island, South Carolina, is a quiet, oceanside retreat for a family of five designed by Anderson Studio. A careful coordination of color and materials encourages the home to harmonize with the surrounding landscape. This project was the recipient of the South Carolina American Institute of Architects Robert Mills Honor Award for Excellence in Residential Design. Photo © 2013 Dana Hoff Photography.

Nestled into a beachfront stand of maritime oaks and designed to embrace one spectacular tree, the overall size of the structure is downplayed by revealing the home in layers, through subtle yet complex architectural solutions.
Photo © 2013 Dana Hoff Photography.

The main living areas flow out onto a sprawling pool deck nestled into the dunes overlooking the Atlantic. Deep overhanging eaves of stained tongue and groove wood provide shade from the intense southern sun. Photo © 2013 Dana Hoff Photography.

In the great room, a color palette inspired by the sand and sea beyond harmonizes with the spectacular view of the Atlantic. The architectural design ensured the maximum unobstructed view through expansive windows and French doors. Richly layered moldings and millwork details subtly encourage a sense of timelessness and historicism. Photo © 2013 Dana Hoff Photography.

Generous banks of window seats envelop the dining room, inviting lingering after-dinner conversations and extended leisurely contemplation of the view beyond. The light cuts of the window design accentuate the sky without obscuring the view of the dune landscape and ocean waters. Photo © 2013 Dana Hoff Photography.

The sculptural quality of the curving stair is expressed through the wall paneling pattern, celebrated with the round lantern pendant, and echoed in the volute newel return detail. A bank of windows at the upper level of the stair turret allows generous natural light to spill in during the daytime and creates a lantern-like effect at night.
Photo © 2013 Dana Hoff Photography.

Large banks of doors disappear to create an effortless linkage between the library and the outdoor living room. A similar material palette of warm wood, stone, and natural woven textures further blurs the dividing line between interior and exterior spaces.
Photo © 2013 Dana Hoff Photography.

Reclaimed river cypress forms a focal point for the kitchen on the island surface, inviting company to join the cook. Full-inlay cabinetry with turned legs, decorative toe kicks, and grain-bin pulls become highly customized furniture-grade accouterments for the room. Soapstone perimeter countertops, glossy subway tile backsplashes, and a custom hood complete the elegant restrained palette.
Photo © 2013 Dana Hoff Photography.

The serene master bath has a spectacular view. Layers of inviting texture are created through the use of varied wood paneling on wall and ceiling surfaces, softly tailored window coverings, polished nickel fittings, and elegant honed marble. Photo © 2013 Dana Hoff Photography.

Nautical-inspired touches make the bunkroom shipshape, with custom built-in berths and canvas accents adding to the casual appeal. Photo © 2013 Dana Hoff Photography.

Timeless tones of sand and sea dress this dormer bedroom. Making the most of balmy ocean breezes, an exquisite reproduction fan accentuates the vaulted ceiling. Photo © 2013 Dana Hoff Photography.

The Creekside Cottage

Built as a refuge for a busy couple, this 4,300 square-foot Shingle Style creekside cottage was constructed on land populated with ancient live oaks. Anderson Studio's designers paid careful attention to locating the building footprint, which preserved the oaks while allowing the volumes to nestle beneath the tranquil canopy. This project was the recipient of the South Carolina American Institute of Architects Robert Mills Honor Award for Excellence in Residential Design. Photo © 2013 Holger Obenaus Photography LLC.

Marsh views are enjoyed from the rear pool deck, the spacious deep screened porches, and the rounded dining room. Deep overhangs provide cool shade and filtered light for the protected spaces.
Photo © 2013 Holger Obenaus Photography LLC.

African sandstone copings, ipe decks, and walls of Venetian plaster and cedar shake combine to create an arresting counterpoint to the natural abundance of the marsh landscape.
Photo © 2013 Holger Obenaus Photography LLC.

Generous openings in the cedar shake walls frame views over the pool to the marsh beyond. Screening, ceiling fans, and cushioned wicker seating ensure year-round comfort in this exterior living room. Photo © 2013 Holger Obenaus Photography LLC.

The vaulted great room is refined yet relaxed, with a palette of soft neutrals grounded by natural textures. The simple wood paneling system sets off the focal points of the room, such as the "thickened thresholds" created by the entry from the foyer beyond and the reading nook with elliptical window and built-in bench flanking the fireplace. Photo © 2013 Holger Obenaus Photography LLC.

The cherry-paneled den serves as a masculine retreat. Built-in window seats flank the fireplace lined in Iguana granite. Substantial cherry beams create handsome coffers, with khaki paint on the ceiling surfaces lending additional warmth to the cozy space. Photo © 2013 Holger Obenaus Photography LLC.

The round dining room element projects out into the landscape, immersing its inhabitants in beautiful marsh views. Expansive windows frame the ancient maritime oaks surrounding the pool deck. The ambiguity of the connection between interior and exterior spaces is furthered by the beautiful blue paint color, which blurs the distinction between wall and water. Photo © 2013 Holger Obenaus Photography LLC.

This bathing alcove in the master bath is cantilevered into the embrace of an existing live oak. Richly stained wood paneling, polished nickel fixtures, heavily veined Amazon Green granite, and intricately patterned travertine combine into a quiet palette for relaxed soaking. Photo © 2013 Holger Obenaus Photography LLC.

The Treehouse

The Anderson Studio designers carefully sited this 4,600 square-foot low country vernacular-inspired tree house on Kiawah Island, South Carolina, in order to take full advantage of spectacular marsh views and crisp ocean breezes. Contemporary detailing of the architectural masses and the landscape provide an updated approach to casual living amidst nature. A restrained color and material palette encourages the design to blend into the natural environment that surrounds it. Photo © 2013 Holger Obenaus Photography LLC.

Adjacent to the master bedroom suite, a hot tub with waterfall invites relaxed contemplation of spectacular marsh sunsets. The incorporation of a living tree into the deck design is an example of the careful consideration and integration of the landscape with the built volume, resulting in an interdependent site-referential design. Photo © 2013 Holger Obenaus Photography LLC.

The separate living and sleeping structures of the Treehouse are connected by a bridging element, suspended over a hardscape-covered pool terrace. The infinity-edged pool allows water to spill over the horizon line, visually and experientially blending with the marsh beyond. Grass-interplanted pavers echo the geometry of the window divisions in the bridge above, quietly reinforcing the architectural language established throughout the project. Photo © 2013 Holger Obenaus Photography LLC.

The gabled great room is lined on all surfaces by warm natural wood and looks out to the surrounding marsh from three expansive window-walls. This great room design was the recipient of the South Carolina American Institute of Architects Robert Mills Honor Citation for Excellence in Residential Design. Photo © 2013 Holger Obenaus Photography LLC.

The walls on the front facade of the Treehouse structure are solid, providing privacy, but they open to rooms of glass, timber, and soaring ceilings with views of Bass and Cinder creeks and Folly Island. Photo © 2013 Holger Obenaus Photography LLC.

A rich wooden wall puts a contemporary spin on a traditional louvered wooden screen and wraps the master suite entry sequence in quiet refinement. Photo © 2013 Holger Obenaus Photography LLC.

An entire wall of glass creates the sensation of showering in the outdoors, while glowing marble and sparkling polished bath fixtures accent the surrounding surfaces. Photo © 2013 Holger Obenaus Photography LLC.

The open plan of the Treehouse allows for spatial flow between the kitchen, dining room, and great room. A consistent palette of warm natural wood, stone, and plaster further unifies the spaces, encouraging a serene aesthetic experience inspired by the surrounding nature. Photo © 2013 Holger Obenaus Photography LLC.

BERCY CHEN STUDIO LP

AUSTIN, TEXAS

Partners Thomas Bercy and Calvin Chen founded Bercy Chen Studio LP, an architecture and urban planning firm with design/build capabilities, in 2001. At Bercy Chen Studio LP, we are committed to collaborating with clients in identifying design solutions and planning strategies to create innovative designs based on environmentally sustainable and financially viable business models in both the public and private sector. Our experience as a design/build operation and our firsthand knowledge of construction and finance are crucial in ensuring successful project implementation.

Thomas is from Belgium, and Calvin is from Taiwan by way of Australia; the European and Asian backgrounds of our partners form a design philosophy of unique perspectives. Our work is influenced by vernacular precedents from various cultures—whether Islamic, Indian, African, or pre-Columbian—and maintains respect for the particular contemporary contextual conditions.

Because of this unique approach, our work has received national and international attention. Bercy Chen Studio won the prestigious "Emerging Voices" prize from the Architectural League of New York in 2006. In the same year, our firm was profiled in *Architectural Record's* December 2006 "Design Vanguard" award issue, as one of top ten emerging design firms in the world. The firm is a member of the City of Austin's Green Building Program and USGBC with certified 3 Star projects.

1111 E 11th St. #200 | Austin, TX 78702
512-481-0092 | www.bcarc.com

Annie House

Bercy Chen designed Annie House for two families in Austin; therefore, it is split into two living areas. The house consists of two pavilions connected by a glass hallway. Since sustainable principles are incorporated throughout the design, the house is a certified City of Austin Green Building, scoring three stars.

The body of water and the spatial continuity between inside and outside were inspired by Asian architecture.

The design was greatly influenced by different regions and cultures. Both the use of the roof as an outdoor living space and the shading devices are derived from Moorish architecture.

The structural transparency of the volumes and the minimalist aspect of the interior were derived from Japanese pavilions.

The house is constructed of a modular steel frame. The frame is in filled with prefab thermal steel panels to minimize construction on-site waste. The structural frame is exposed, showing the construction process and articulating the house's facades.

The repetitive modular method, as well as the prefabrication, allowed for greater efficiency during construction.

ANNIE HOUSE

Cascading Creek House

Bercy Chen conceived the Cascading Creek House less as a house, but more as an extension and outgrowth of the limestone and aquifers of the Central Texas geography.

The roof structure is configured so as to create a natural basin for the collection of rainwater, not unlike the vernal pools found in the outcroppings of Enchanted Rock. These basins harness additional natural flows through the use of photovoltaic and solar hot-water panels.

CASCADING CREEK HOUSE

The water, electricity, and heat harvested on the roof tie into an extensive climate conditioning system that utilizes water source, heat pumps, and radiant loops to supply both the heating and cooling for the residence.

The climate system is connected to geothermal ground loops as well as pools and water features, thereby establishing a system of heat exchange that minimizes reliance on electricity or gas.

The primary formal gesture of the project inserts two long native limestone walls into the site. The walls serve as the boundary marking domesticated space. The vegetation outside of these walls is native while the interior spaces are more lush and tropical.

The program of the residence is configured along the stone walls. Each serves as the spine for the public and private wings, respectively.

The offset between the main wings establishes an exterior courtyard that will serve as an extended living space for much of the year.

Three mature native oaks inform the siting of the boundary walls and building elements.

Peninsula House

Featured in the New York Times, Milan Daily News, and Vision Beijing, this Bercy Chen residence was originally a 1980s homebuilder home fronting Lake Austin.

The existing house was a typical American wood stud framing building, which is often demolished to make way for a brand new structure. Nevertheless, after some consideration, the owner decided to keep the existing "bones" and completely re-organize the house.

Through the use of glass, steel, detailing, and lighting, the project sought to update the home's interior while redefining its relationship with the lake beyond.

A glass solarium with the same roof angle is created, rotated 20 degrees in plan to follow the side property line, creating a new triangular pool and lap pool extending to the boathouse.

The strategy for re-designing this residence was to use reflective surfaces such as acrylic panels and mirrors on walls and doors parallel to the lake, thereby picking up the subtle reflection of the light and water's rippling motion on the walls as a subtle way to acknowledge the lake side location. The idea is to treat architectural elements as minimalist installation art to interact with nature.

Existing dormer window were extended vertically to create a large opening for natural light; this niche can also become a space for reading. Red acrylic panels are lit from behind, and the effect is a red slit opening against the massaranduba bench, which wraps around the angled wall.

A vegetated roof mitigates the water quality impact of the intervention, while serving as a test bed for residential green roofs in sub-tropical climates.

MARLON BLACKWELL ARCHITECT

FAYETTEVILLE, ARKANSAS

Marlon Blackwell Architect is a design-centered, critical practice of nine people located in Fayetteville, Arkansas. By seeking out the immutable qualities of each place, we find solutions that are specific and thus resistant to commercialization, not dependent on any style but responsive to culture, climate, and context. This is, in a way, an act of resistance, a refusal to accept less than what we believe possible and one that sees the world as a source of rich opportunity.

We have built a reputation for producing award-winning and environmentally responsive architectural projects since our inception in 1990. Originally known for the iconic TowerHouse and Honeyhouse, we have built upon the principles of those projects—sensitive siting, the significance of experience, and attention to detail and materials—to develop an array of original and significant projects that range from that same residential scale to large public works including urban planning.

As a result, we have earned a national and international design reputation through recognition of our work in many publications, including architectural design journals and books, and more than 70 state, regional, national, and international design awards. The American Academy of Arts and Letters recognized us with an Architecture Prize in 2012, and the Princeton Architectural Press published a monograph entitled *An Architecture of the Ozarks: The Works of Marlon Blackwell.*

217 East Dickson Street, Suite 104 | Fayetteville, AR 72701
479-973-9121 | info@marlonblackwell.com | www.marlonblackwell.com

Arkansas House

The challenge for Marlon Blackwell was to introduce possibilities for re-thinking the spatial character of a fire-damaged house. The firm had three weeks to design its interventions and resolved details after construction began. It was allowed to work only in the fire-damaged zones of the existing house (exterior and interior), leaving the remainder untouched beyond new windows and a new HVAC system. Today, Corten steel monitors lined in cherry veneer plywood sit gently atop the original white masonry structure, overlooking the wooded ravine below. Courtesy of Timothy Hursley.

Nestled in the woods atop a rocky ledge, the living room and a covered porch are surrounded by the trees. Courtesy of Timothy Hursley.

Custom steel and hardwood handrails line the mezzanine that overlooks the living room and woods beyond. Courtesy of Timothy Hursley.

The firm's tactic was to float cherry and walnut veneer panels over the pier walls and along the ceiling forming a detached interior skin. Flooring of rift-sawn cherry and walnut also act to form an interior liner. The mezzanine looks inward to the living room below and out to the surrounding forest. Courtesy of Timothy Hursley.

The great room is naturally lit from all sides and fills the center of the house with light and views to the sky and adjacent monitors above. An art wall of custom Corten steel shingles floats inside the room. Courtesy of Timothy Hursley.

The living room and mezzanine above project into the nearby woods. Courtesy of Timothy Hursley.

L-Stack House

The L-Stack House responds to a site anomaly set within a dense inner city neighborhood near a city park. A dry bed creek traverses the 10,000 square-foot trapezoid-shaped lot diagonally. Marlon Blackwell enhanced the urban grid and the modest scale of existing houses in the neighborhood through a strategy of bridging and stacking of forms. In effect, a new order is superimposed upon an in-fill tract of land that has been undeveloped since the nineteenth century origins of the city of Fayetteville. The resulting scheme is an "L" configuration that subdivides the interior program and the site into private and public entities. Courtesy of Timothy Hursley.

Resting gently above the front door, the bedroom wing projects to create a front porch and stoop. Courtesy of Timothy Hursley.

The ground floor is organized as a linear open plan with connecting terraces along and adjacent to the creek. The living room, kitchen, and dining rooms flow together in the "bridge" above the creek, sharing light from windows and skylights. Throughout the house, windows and skylights are arranged to provide controlled views, illumination, a sense of privacy, and opportunities to observe the dynamic nature of the creek. Courtesy of Timothy Hursley.

L-STACK HOUSE

Private spaces are more discreet and cellular; however, all spaces open onto a hall that serves as a common family space for reading, office work, or watching television. Primary interior materials include teak floors, wenge, walnut, and white oak millwork, and painted wood plank accent walls. Large steel box windows provide spaces for sitting or sleeping. Courtesy of Timothy Hursley.

A carefully positioned glass-enclosed stairway hinges together the two 18-foot wide boxes that form the house structure. One side of the stairway is clear and open to the landscape behind the house while the other side is translucent for privacy from the nearby neighbors. Courtesy of Timothy Hursley.

The exterior cladding is a unique rain screen system articulated with rot resistant Brazilian redwood. The wood screen is disengaged from a rubber-clad substrate and is stacked and screwed on the flat, creating a horizontal, louvered effect at the long walls. The cladding system provides for 50 percent transparency and perceptually provides the walls with a phenomenal translucency. End walls are either black metal clad or glass storefronts. A large covered terrace sits streamside below the bedroom wing above. Courtesy of Timothy Hursley.

TowerHouse

As a child, the owner spent many memorable days and nights in a tree house built by his grandfather. In homage to these memories, he requested that Marlon Blackwell design a vertical structure that would rise above the 50-foot high tree canopy and provide panoramic views of the surrounding Ozark mountain landscape. The exterior of the Towerhouse is clad in local white oak and industrial metal panels, referencing the trees on site and white agricultural buildings nearby. Courtesy of Timothy Hursley.

The northwest corner of the tower is illuminated from within, revealing several smaller windows that frame views during the ascent. Courtesy of Timothy Hursley.

All mechanical, plumbing, and electrical lines are channeled through one vertical chase wall that also serves as structure for a small dumbwaiter. A refined hardwood stair leads the final few steps to the living room inside the top of the tower. Courtesy of Timothy Hursley.

TOWERHOUSE

The (82.33 ft.) high tower structure functions as a residential retreat with programmed levels including a utility room, foyer/bathroom/kitchenette, living/sleeping room (el. 57.00 ft.), and a sky court for outdoor dining and observation. A table folds out from the west wall of the sky court for outdoor dining. White oak slats line the interior of the sky deck. Courtesy of Timothy Hursley.

The continuous steel frame windows (7-1/2 ft.), provide 360-degree views of the surrounding landscape. Courtesy of Timothy Hursley.

CARTER+BURTON ARCHITECTURE PLC

BERRYVILLE, VIRGINIA

A Virginia architecture firm, we specialize in a few good projects per year. Located in Berryville, a small town one hour west of Washington, DC, our architects love to design and work with people, and are committed to doing modern work within a wide range of budgets. The firm's focus is on quality, craftsmanship, and innovation and in promoting passive solar techniques and eco-friendly building materials.

11 W. Main St. | Berryville, VA 22611
540-955-1644 | jim@carterburton.com | www.carterburton.com

Elk Run

The Carter+Burton designed house is anchored by gravity fieldstone walls of the master bedroom wing and a chimney at the northern end of the living room volume. A regional response to the southern climate, the house design features a dogtrot dividing the main house from guest studio, porches with generous overhangs, and a screened porch appropriate to large family gatherings. Courtesy of Russell Abraham Photography.

The entry court to Elk Run Ridge is bounded by a water feature, which captures rainwater from the roof and the gravity fieldstone wall of the master bedroom wing. A local artisan handcrafted the front door. Courtesy of Russell Abraham Photography.

Anchoring the opposite end of the house, the fieldstone chimney serves spaces inside and outside at the dogtrot. The concrete floors were polished to a museum quality finish. Glulams and massive columns contribute to the open space that reaches beyond to the outdoors. Courtesy of Russell Abraham Photography.

The basket weave walls wrap the core functions from the master bath to the kitchen and can be seen from the main living space. A custom stainless steel hood was fabricated to fit in the tall space of the great room. This "instant heirloom" home was built to showcase the owner's many Nakashima pieces. Courtesy of Russell Abraham Photography.

A study in material expression, the master bedroom features plaster walls, exposed fieldstone, cedar and fir ceiling, and a walnut basket weave headboard wall. The sliver windows under the glulam beams provide light and privacy in the massive walls.
Courtesy of Russell Abraham Photography

The zinc standing seam metal roof folds on the north side to protect the house from storms. The studio and guest rooms float above the landscape with surrounding deck. Large lift and slide doors open up the interior to views of the hills of the Blue Ridge Mountains.
Courtesy of Russell Ab·aham Photography.

Pond View

The geometries of the existing assembly of farm buildings have provided a unique approach to the new house designed by Carter+Burton. This is heightened by the layout of the house as it slides towards the pond to capture views of the pond. Old materials such as standing seam metal and wood siding are used in new ways in stark contrast to the century-old buildings. Courtesy of Russell Abraham Photography.

The house massing is expressed with differentiated volumes for the public and private zones. The wood and stone bedroom volume completes the "Modern Barnyard" court, and the steel-framed living space steps lightly near the fragile bank of the pond. Courtesy of Russell Abraham Photography.

Large windows capture the main view of the pond. Engineered overhangs protect the house from getting too warm from sun exposure in the summer. Extremely well insulated with tight construction including spray foam insulation and SIPs and geothermal heat pumps, the owners enjoy energy expenses of less than $40 a month. Courtesy of Russell Abraham Photography.

The owner's favorite spot to sip a cup of tea or play the clarinet, the main level deck overlooks the pond while also being protected from sun and rain. Courtesy of Russell Abraham Photography.

The unexpected roof deck and green roof further insulate the house. A bird's eye retreat, the owners can see all of their farm and the surrounding hillsides. Courtesy of Russell Abraham Photography.

One of the owners built the kitchen cabinets, the stair treads, and the front door in his woodshop on site. The other owner is a prolific painter and displays her vibrant art throughout the home. The loft above the dining room and kitchen is a library retreat. The lower ceiling creates a more intimate setting for meals. Courtesy of Russell Abraham Photography.

GLAVÈ & HOLMES ARCHITECTURE

RICHMOND, VIRGINIA

The Home Studio at Glavè & Holmes Architecture, under the leadership of Gary Inman, is a well-balanced team of experienced architects and designers, each with particular strengths and depth of expertise. In our relationship within the firm, we are like a chamber group within a symphony, specializing in the most intensely personal kind of design. The dialogue between designer and client is critical to the underlying design idea, and we listen intently to discover those values, tastes, and aspirations that will lead us to the finished project. No detail of function or finish escapes our attention.

Our houses give us shelter, privacy, and places to put things, but they are so much more. A house designed or renovated or enlarged with care and attention to every detail supports and cooperates with the way we spend our days, and the way our family life is lived. It is a welcome citizen of its neighborhood or region. It surrounds us with the colors we love and the belongings that delight us and hold our history. It gives us a sense of personal satisfaction, of self-expression, and of peace, becoming in every sense a home. This is the aspiration of our team. We believe that design, at its best, is a language that describes the life journey of the client, interpreted with the fluency of our experience.

2101 East Main St. | Richmond, VA 23223
804-649-9303 | ginman@glaveandholmes.com | www.glaveandholmes.com

Distinctly English

This distinctly English stone home, while just completed in 2012, has the bearing and sensibility of a century-old English manor. Inspired by the work of the venerated English architect, Charles Voysey, Glavè & Holmes and Wallace Architecture minimalized the Tudor bones, which are counterbalanced by a French tower that serves as a two-story library.

This home was designed and built over a 4-year period in the New York area. Gary Inman was the lead designer for Glavè & Holmes Architecture who did the interior architecture and the interior design. The project was in collaboration with Skip Wallace of Wallace Architects. The design team included Gary Inman, Skip Wallace, Mindy Carter, Jennifer Rhoades, Eleanor Barton, J.B. Elko, Veronica Ledford, and Catherine Stanley. Photo courtesy of Ansel Olson.

The handcrafted door of oak and hand-forged ironwork permits a graceful arrival. Artisan-made glass with lead cames recalls the spirit of the Arts & Crafts Movement as does the bespoke Sebastian Settle (bench) by Gary Inman and Joseph Elko. Photo courtesy of Ansel Olson.

The music room hosts a meticulously restored vintage Steinway piano, circa 1917, and a collection of small prints and etchings by Moses Soyer and several nineteenth century French artists. Hand-embroidered sage green linen from Chelsea Textiles adorns the windows and compliments the Farrow & Ball powder blue walls. Photo courtesy of Ansel Olson.

The great hall affords a stately point of arrival befitting this well-crafted English-inspired home. The overall neutral palette of limestone, painted plate-rail height paneling, and geometric balustrade is punctuated by the dark tones of mahogany or oak. An antique Federal period chest and èglomisè mirror adds character of age. Photo courtesy of Ansel Olson.

English Tudor paneling and South Carolina cypress are paired and served up in the dining room. Crewelwork draperies, creil plates, cast plaster, and a hand-forged fretwork chandelier charge the room with the energy of the artisan's hand. A still life by French artist Alix Aymè, a favorite of the client, sets the tone for the space. Photo courtesy of Ansel Olson.

The tower library and spiral staircase celebrate the craftsmanship of both blacksmith and cabinet-maker. African mahogany blends with American walnut flooring and butternut, which lines the bookcases. The focal point, nonetheless, is the hand-crafted steel staircase inspired by plate 849 of Macfarlane's Castings, Vol. 1 of 1882, brilliantly executed by a local blacksmith. Photo courtesy of Ansel Olson.

Designed as the center of family activity and informal entertaining, this painted and glazed kitchen is cozy but efficient with an adjoining pantry for additional storage. Soapstone counters, oak flooring, and a cerused oak ceiling add warmth to the cream and celadon color scheme. Photo courtesy of Ansel Olson.

The sink alcove affords a view of the wooded landscape and the chance to converse with guests on the screened dining porch. The sink is hammered pewter with a bridge style faucet. The scale of the sink makes it a wonderful place for arranging flowers. Photo courtesy of Ansel Olson.

Serene luxury was the guiding aspiration that shaped this tranquil alcove. Healing aloe (Benjamin Moore) walls, a Waterworks soaking tub, Christie's linens, hand-embroidered window treatments, and a hand-cut and set marble mosaic floor add a bespoke quality to this space. Photo courtesy of Ansel Olson.

Timeless elegance was the goal for this guest bath featuring a marble floor, English wallpaper and a high wainscoting. A caned chair and needlepoint cushion add a feminine touch. Photo courtesy of Ansel Olson.

Repose at Montalto

Repose is a Virginia country house, circa 1905, built on the highest mountain in Albemarle County with views of nearby Monticello, home of Thomas Jefferson, and the city of Charlottesville. Glavè & Holmes Architecture was commissioned to restore and enlarge the historic home. Today, the facade has a coat of vivid orange Ludowici terracotta tile. The Albemarle green stone and muscular columns anchor the house to the ground while the pergola and balconies add lightness, a juxtaposition often found in houses of this period. Photo courtesy of Ansel Olson.

Garden facade of the house showing the stone terraces and the newly expanded conservatory. Photo courtesy of Ansel Olson.

Beside the original front door are fretwork benches, a Jeffersonian element. McLean Lighting in North Carolina crafted the lanterns. Photo courtesy of Ansel Olson.

The main parlor offers multiple seating areas and a chance to cozy up by the fire. The walls are Hancock Green, a historic color from Benjamin Moore, and pair handsomely with the period-inspired toile at the windows. A portrait of Thomas Jefferson surveys the room from the over mantle. Photo courtesy of Ansel Olson.

Main entrance hall and staircase with the adjoining parlor to the right. A period photograph of the space inspired the carpet, Chinese garden stool, and curly maple bench. Photo courtesy of Ansel Olson.

Every home deserves a conservatory, a perfect blending of indoor and outdoor space. The camel back sofas were fabricated in Virginia by McKinnon & Harris, tables from Gary Inman Home Couture, and dining chairs from Andrew Crace, England. Photo courtesy of Ansel Olson.

A number of the original furnishings were located and brought back to the mountaintop. The print collection shows three of Thomas Jefferson's architectural masterpieces along with the prototypes that inspired them. Photo courtesy of Ansel Olson.

A lady's dressing room with Carrera marble and hand-painted Welsh tiles recall a more graceful era. The custom vanity sits atop a period-style octagonal tile floor with cobalt accents. Photo courtesy of Ansel Olson.

GUYON ARCHITECTS INCORPORATED/THE STUDIO FOR ARCHITECTURE

LEXINGTON, KENTUCKY

Guyon Architects / The Studio for Architecture was founded in 1985 as a multi-disciplinary firm dedicated to the practice of studio architecture.

Studio architecture is defined and structured by the belief that architecture is a poetic, spatial art form. Working under this belief demands that we delve as deeply as possible into every aspect of every project that comes under our guidance, regardless of size or scope.

Architecture has the power to enhance, enable, and transform every human activity. This fundamental belief drives us relentlessly toward designing space of the highest possible quality for those who will occupy it—within the boundaries of schedule, budget, and technology.

If awards are measures of success, the American Institute of Architects (AIA) has honored Guyon Architects with eleven awards for Excellence in Architectural Design since 1988—more than any other architecture firm in the history of AIA awards in Kentucky. They are awards for the design of residences to large projects such as banks

Prior to entering architecture school, Guyon spent several years in Chicago at the firm of Powell / Kleinschmidt Architects, working closely with Skidmore, Owings and Merrill. After earning his degree (with honors) in architecture from the University of Kentucky in 1983, Guyon decided that his vision of "integral architecture" could best be developed in the Bluegrass Region of Kentucky. He founded the Studio for Architecture in 1985 and joined the faculty of the University of Kentucky's College of Architecture the following year. He was honored with the AIAS/AIA award for Outstanding Practitioner in Education and the 1999 Silver Medal.

401 West Main St. Suite 321 | Lexington, KY 40507
guyon-design@msn.com | www.guyonarchitects.com

A House in Horse Country

It seems possible that a house can embody a narrative story as well as fulfilling less lofty notions. This 3,800 square-foot residence is located in horse country along a tall ridge that runs next to the Kentucky River. The site provides a stunning "50 mile" view.

Designed by Guyon Architects, the house is inspired by both the rock fences of this region and the common tractor sheds that are seen often on the hillsides of local farms. This view is of the south elevation.

View of the south elevation at dusk

The stone walls were laid from small pieces, thus "weaving" a surface that gains a fabric-like quality. These are set against oak floors and maple cabinetry. The exterior is a combination of metal barn roof, bleached cedar, steel columns, and stone walling.

This house has been placed along a south-facing ridge with the intention of greeting the visitor from the road to the North and opening to the sky toward the South. Its real desire is to reconcile the tough beauty of a barn with the intricacy of modern architecture.

It seems possible that a house can embody a narrative story as well as fulfilling less lofty notions. This 3,800 square-foot residence is located in horse country along a tall ridge that runs next to the Kentucky River. The site provides a stunning "50 mile" view.

View of the master suite.

The Undulation of Roofs

As the architect for this 2000 square-foot residence, Guyon's early sketches aspired toward a world of "two's": up and down, solid and void, communal and solitary, among others. The 10-acre site is located in the rolling landscape of western Woodford county less than a mile from the Kentucky River. The owner simply asked for daylight, views of nature, and a painting studio.

The plan is governed by the adjacency of two "sheds," which are joined by a central wall that has a hand-laid limestone base with barn-metal cladding above. The two shed structures are positioned with opposing slopes to one another. This allows the western shed, containing the main living area, to open vertically to the southwestern view. The painting studio, located in the eastern shed, receives the northerly "artist's light." The undulation of the two roof slopes permits the main sleeping room to benefit from a wide vista and simultaneously shelter itself at a lower height to gain a sense of security.

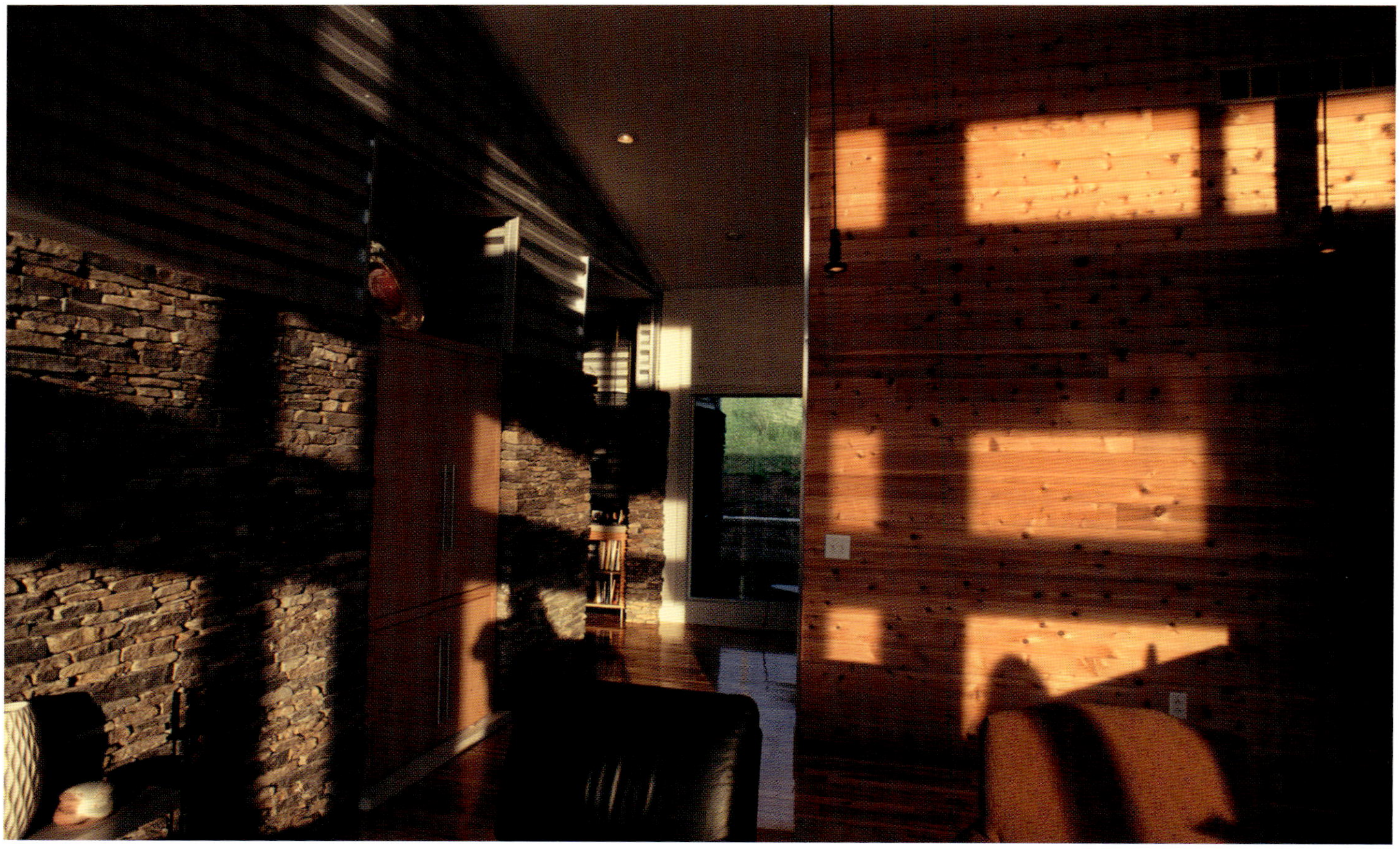

The predominant exterior wood is bleached cedar with the soffit areas continuously covered in varnished spruce. The remaining exterior elements are flat-stacked limestone, metal barn-roofing, and steel columns. Maple cabinetry, birch doors, and birch flooring comprise the interior materials.

View of the house looking northeast at dusk.

MARK HAMPTON, FAIA

MIAMI, FLORIDA

Strongly influenced by Mies van der Rohe, the architecture I have strived to produce is minimal in its structural expression, yet humanely scaled and meticulously detailed. Ultimately informed by my client's program, my work is characterized by its clarity of function and circulation, the logic of its special relationships, and the precise selection of appropriate materials.

3900 Loquat Avenue Miami, FL 31333
305-443-6945

Tropical Paradise

Mark Hampton's clients were entranced with the dense tropical vegetation that blanketed their two-acre plot of land in a quiet neighborhood. They wanted a house that would be open to the outside rather than shut away. They wanted a user-friendly home that would allow them to entertain easily. To allow for easy interaction between the rooms, Hampton placed rooms on different levels, using small sets of steps to connect them. The 18-inch stairs can also act as seats during large gatherings. The lack of doors encourages fluidity during large receptions; the walls give visual privacy. Photo © Steven Brooke.

The design reflects Hampton's minimalist bent. Many of the rooms have white stucco walls and oak ceilings with black aluminum window frames and fans. Dun-colored Mexican tiles cover the floors. Photo © Steven Brooke.

The house is punctuated with huge windows and skylights that draw in Florida's abundant natural plant life. Photo © Steven Brooke.

Outside the kitchen, a weathered redwood deck contains a 75-foot lap pool lined in black tiles. The use of black tiles, rather than the standard blue, de-emphasizes the pool. Photo © Steven Brooke.

Bachelor Pavilion

This Hampton house is reminiscent of Mies van Der Rohe's steel-framed, glass houses for the tropics. The white gravel courtyard leads to a 56-foot-long rectangle punctuated by a series of white brick cylinders and half circles that contain a kitchen and bathroom. Photo © Steven Brooke.

The dominant feature of the living room is a semi-circular conversation pit in front of a raised hearth. The floor is covered in terrazzo and marble; the ceiling paneled in pecan; and the main furniture is built in. Photo © Steven Brooke.

BACHELOR PAVILION

House of Circles

One of Hampton's distinctive characteristics is the way in which his buildings frame views, whether it is the skyline, nature, or water. Courtesy of George A. Cott.

Mark Hampton's style is distinguished by his awareness of the interplay between interior space and nature. Courtesy of George A. Cott.

The library also doubles as an intimate dining room. Bookshelves line the circular walls. The color of the volumes contrast with the white textured Carrera marble flooring used throughout the first floor. Courtesy of George A. Cott.

Hampton likes geometric themes. Straight lines interplay with circles, contrasting with the Florida landscape. Courtesy of George A. Cott.

FRANK HARMON ARCHITECT PA

RALEIGH, NORTH CAROLINA

We are a client-based design practice. The story of our projects, whether a 70,000-square-foot corporate headquarters or a playhouse for children, is told through the conversations we have with our clients and the particular chemistry of the sites upon which we build. The results are portraits of our clients, as diverse and individual as they are.

Underpinning our practice are professionalism and sustainability in the widest sense. We work as a relatively small, close-knit team with a carefully chosen number of projects, enabling us to offer an exceptional level of service to our clients. Our work has won fifty-five design awards and is published internationally.

We recently moved our office to the AIA NC Center for Architecture and Design at 14 East Peace Street in downtown Raleigh, a building we designed as a competition in 2008, completed in 2012, and intended as a sustainable workplace. It is the beginning of a new chapter in the life of our practice, one that seeks to bring good architecture to a broader public.

14 East Peace St. | Raleigh, NC 27604
919-829-9464 | www.frankharmon.com

Accommodating Nature

This modern home, designed by Frank Harmon on Shem Creek, welcomes nature and protects against it. Its long, one-room-deep floor plan gives each room windows and porches overlooking Shem Creek. Bedrooms are located on opposite ends of the central, loft-like living/dining/kitchen area, beneath a single shed roof. Courtesy of Richard Leo Johnson/Atlantic Archives, Inc.

The homeowner wanted an abundance of windows overlooking the creek. That presented two challenges: sun would bake in from that direction, and flying debris would threaten the house during hurricanes. Frank Harmon's solution: a series of 10 hand-fabricated metal screens hinged above the porch to protect this vulnerable face from summer sun and extreme weather, while allowing cooling breezes into the house. By design, a single person can manipulate the screens. Courtesy of Richard Leo Johnson/Atlantic Archives, Inc.

The 800-pound metal screens in their "down" position create a shaded porch behind them and keep hurricane-blown debris from breaking the glass wall. Courtesy of Richard Leo Johnson/Atlantic Archives, Inc.

Natural light and ventilation fill the central living/dining/kitchen area, which overlooks the creek and a lap pool that runs parallel to the creek. Courtesy of Richard Leo Johnson/Atlantic Archives, Inc.

A ramp under a canopy of moss-draped live oaks leads to the house. The view of the marsh beyond the house appears like an element in a Japanese painting. Courtesy of Richard Leo Johnson/Atlantic Archives, Inc.

Color Me Home

A married couple—he, an architect, she, a landscape architect—designed their modern dream home and gardens simultaneously. The couple's house and gardens were designed as halves of the greater "whole"—as equal parts of the living experience. The house designed by Frank Harmon rests on concrete piers to protect the roots of mature trees that shade the house's abundant windows. The gardens' curvilinear design by Judy Harmon creates a paisley of sunny, open spaces and dense, shaded foliage. They were carefully planted to offer something to see and enjoy from inside the house year-round.
Courtesy of Tom Aldi Photography.

Walls and fences provide privacy and the perfect foil for climbing vines. Color provides vibrancy that's echoed by the gardens' foliage. Courtesy of Tom Aldi Photography.

Wrap-around windows in the kitchen/dining area frame views of the gardens and maintain constant visual contact with the outdoors.
Courtesy of Tom Aldi Photography.

The central, two-story clean living space flows into the dining/kitchen area (left, facing the front wall) and a lower-ceilinged sunroom overlooking the pool (right). Bedrooms and a balcony are on the second level. To give the house a sense of both strength and lightness, the couple used steel for the structure and an abundance of glass.
Courtesy of Tom Aldi Photography.

The swimming pool projects from the east side of the house. Outer walls extend the living room into the gardens. The colors of the house and pool are cheerful and complement zinnias, yuccas, and palm trees growing in the gardens.
Courtesy of Tom Aldi Photography.

Reach For The Sky

This hillside home designed by Frank Harmon celebrates the owner's request for "something dramatic." Topped by a metal "butterfly" roof, the house seems poised to take flight. A bridge leads to the entrance level. A private outdoor deck is located beneath the bridge. Photo © Jeffrey Jacobs.

The house's rear elevation under the butterfly roof. Notice the broad-shouldered wood trusses that support the house and avoid disturbing the natural hydrology of the steep site. Photo © Jeffrey Jacobs.

Floor-to-ceiling glass on the rear elevation welcomes the natural environment into the house. Of course, the view changes with each season. The glass wall's steel structure, painted a deep gray, mimics the tree trunks outside. Photo © Jeffrey Jacobs

From the balcony-like entrance foyer, a handcrafted steel staircase (left) with wooden treads descends past the glass—in essence, through the trees—to the dramatic, two-story-clear main living floor. The living area flows seamlessly into the dining area and kitchen. Beyond the kitchen are the media room (or second bedroom) and a full bath. A door near the kitchen opens to the private outdoor deck. Photo © Jeffrey Jacobs.

Cherry floors, B&B Italia® and George Nakashima furnishings, and original art work by Raleigh artist Gerry Lynch support the owners' elegant minimalist style, which focuses on texture, light, and materials. Photo © Jeffrey Jacobs.

The master bedroom suite is located on the entrance level so the owners feel as if they're sleeping up in the trees. Note the steel wall that separates the sleep area from the bath and the exposed plywood ceiling. The owner wanted the house to be utterly devoid of unnecessary ornamentation to the point that she could see the marks of construction, from exposed bolts at the metal columns to the "unfinished" ceiling structure. Photo © Jeffrey Jacobs.

McCOLLOUGH ARCHITECTURE, INC.

ORANGE BEACH, ALABAMA

McCollough Architecture, Inc., nestled on the Alabama Gulf Coast in the fishing community of Orange Beach, is a premier architectural firm focused on producing quality, client-centered design solutions within budgetary constraints. Because our firm is located in a coastal region, we walk a tightrope to balance the structural constraints of high wind and potential storm surges while trying to maximize openings to take full advantage of the dramatic views.

Our portfolio includes a diverse list of projects ranging from all styles of residential homes, to larger commercial structures including The Hangout, Kaiser Realty, and Columbia Southern University, and even smaller projects such as the City of Gulf Shores lifeguard towers. We enjoy the wide variety of projects that allow for more creative expression in our design. One of the most rewarding projects we have ever been a part of was designing a home for ABC's "Extreme Home Makeover" in Hattiesburg, Mississippi. To see a community rally around a military family in need was the experience of a lifetime. We feel it is important to maintain a natural aesthetic and utilize strong visual elements ultimately leading to a unique design for each project.

4790 Main St. | Suite F-209 | Orange Beach, AL 36561
251-968-7222 | stedm@mcarcht.com | www.mccollougharchitecture.com

The Captain's Quarters

This minimalistic contemporary home designed by McCollough Architecture located in Orange Beach, Alabama, was inspired by dogtrot-style homes of the nineteenth century. The dogtrot style maximizes ventilation with a courtyard breezeway running through the center of the home. The dining room, located above the pool, serves as the bridge between the two elements of the house. The north side overlooks Bayou St. John. Courtesy of High Seas Design House.

Functionally, the home is very secure, with a lockable courtyard entrance. This door opens into the open-air courtyard to reveal the dogtrot breezeway and pool area, which essentially divides the lower floor level into two parts. Courtesy of High Seas Design House.

The large, open floor plan provides for an efficient kitchen, living and dining area. The clerestory windows, complete with color-changing LED lights, accents the curvilinear ceiling. Courtesy of High Seas Design House.

With a stacked stone accent wall, the living room area features a large, custom fireplace. Joe Rankin of Rankin Interiors in Jackson, Mississippi, was responsible for the interior decorating. The automatic door opens to the upper porch and outdoor kitchen area. Courtesy of High Seas Design House.

McCollough's design provided for floor-to-ceiling windows on either side of the dining room, allowing for spectacular views over the pool below and the front yard. Courtesy of High Seas Design House.

Guest rooms are located on each side of the lower level, as is the main entry foyer to the home. Courtesy of High Seas Design House.

The front corner of the home provides for the towering storefront that showcases the winding glass staircase leading to an open loft overlooking the kitchen and living area. Courtesy of High Seas Design House.

The white stucco exterior, aluminum cladding, metal roof system, and high-grade stainless steel elements create a nautical (and almost ship-like) feel. The ship-like quality is again emphasized with the wrapping of the pool around the edges of the house. Courtesy of High Seas Design House.

The view from the upper porch is reminiscent of the bow of a ship, providing for the perfect place to view sunsets over the bayou. Courtesy of High Seas Design House.

Southern Oaks Estate

Designed by McCollough Architecture, the house features a spacious wrap-around front porch. The low picket fence and landscaping bring the traditional feel of the home to life. Courtesy of Dusty Bias.

This traditional Southern vernacular home is situated on two lots in a golf course community. The pastoral setting looks across the lake to the tee box of a par-3 hole. Courtesy of Dusty Bias.

SOUTHERN OAKS ESTATE

The back of the home has an outdoor living space complete with a dining area, half-bath, fireplace, and mini-kitchen for entertaining guests, as well as a screened-in pool and hot tub. Courtesy of Dusty Bias.

Like any true Southern home, the front porch is equipped with rocking chairs and a porch swing, perfect for that first cup of coffee in the morning. Courtesy of Dusty Bias.

The kitchen has a nine-foot island bar, custom cabinetry, and exposed beams in the ceiling. Courtesy of Dusty Bias.

SOUTHERN OAKS ESTATE

A Breath of Fresh Air

This transitional cottage-style home, a renovation of an old beach house in Orange Beach, Alabama, overlooks Bayou St. John. The addition added approximately 2,000 square feet to the home. Courtesy of High Seas Design House.

One of the many unique features of this home, designed by McCollough Architecture, is the large, split-level entry porch and foyer. Courtesy of High Seas Design House.

With exposed beams and a brick fireplace, the living room is a cozy space with fantastic water views. The fireplace is flanked with a large window on one side and access to a small study on the other. Courtesy of High Seas Design House.

The primary addition includes a new kitchen and living room. It is strategically angled to capture the views overlooking Bayou St. John. Courtesy of High Seas Design House.

The dining room was relocated to overlook the foyer and provides for a large 18-foot square room. Melanie Martin of Orange Beach, Alabama, did the interior design. Courtesy of High Seas Design House.

The redesign and expansion of the master bedroom suite upstairs included a completely renovated master bath and additional windows in the master bedroom. Courtesy of High Seas Design House.

Lajas Mierisch
Gourmet Coffee
Lajas Estate

MOON BROS., INC. ARCHITECTS

ATLANTA, GEORGIA

Moon Bros. Inc. Architects started our practice in 1972 with the philosophy of total dedication to understanding the client's needs and desires and offering creative and effective designs that address these goals. Every project is a one-of-a-kind collaboration between client, architect, and contractor to produce a work of art. Our craftsmen actually construct most of their architectural designs, which allows the quality to telegraph through the completed work. Because each project is unique, our body of work has ranged from very contemporary to mountain lodge to country French and everything in between. Each design is a team effort of one of the founding partners and an architect associate. Attention to detail, love of materials, creative use of light, and the ability to complement the personalities of our clients through architecture in each project has become the hallmark of Moon Bros. Inc. Architects.

1662 McLendon Ave. NE | Atlanta, GA 30307
404-377-6006 | Amanda@MoonBros.com | www.moonbros.com

Subdued Elegance

This surprisingly large house encased in a well-defined, yet demure shell. At 7,800 square feet, the goal of the design by Moon Bros., Inc., was to intentionally keep the house subdued yet elegant. The scale reduction of the mass of the pieces of the building contributes to the graceful, horizontal lines while maintaining the program. Courtesy of Galina Coada.

This detailed photo of the entry to the residence effectively portrays the sloped brick walls with projected, accent corner quoins. The utilization of rain chains in lieu of traditional downspouts accentuate the tapered walls and create an occasional waterfall effect that is much appreciated by the inhabitants. The restrained color palette of the exterior provides a quiet, sophisticated strength to the house. Courtesy of Galina Coada.

Distinct ceiling planes differentiate contiguous spaces in this great room layout. The sculpted ceiling of the living space aids in defining the fireplace elevation as the focal point while providing soft lighting details as the cove light washes over the textured ceiling plane. The rich mosaic texture of the fireplace surround is flanked by smooth mahogany cabinets, which, in turn, are framed by a golden cork wall covering providing layers of stepped finishes. The moveable glass panel walls that connect to the screened porch beyond expand the useful living space of this area. Courtesy of Galina Coada.

Creating an outdoor living, dining, and entertaining space with processional connection to the main house was the goal of this porch and outdoor kitchen. Since this residence is located on a tight, urban site, efficiently utilizing the exterior spaces and providing a connection to the interior while maintaining views was of utmost importance. The increasing openness of the spaces as one approaches the porch creates a feeling of lightness and strengthens the connection to the outside and sky. The brick columns that frame the screened porch confidently exhibit the slope of the exterior wall plane that is present on the entire facade. Courtesy of Galina Coada.

The client-driven details are what make this kitchen unique, yet wholly functional. The top layer of typically forgotten space is utilized for display of a teapot collection. The accent mahogany wood that frames this detail as well as the wood floor inlay that runs throughout the public spaces of this open plan unite the individual spaces. To the left is a glimpse of the ritual sink, a centrally located hand washing station. The island is sized for food preparation as well as for family dinners up to eight. A lot of cooking goes on in this space. Courtesy of Galina Coada.

Moon Bros., Inc., has created an open and expansive bathroom that connects directly to the exterior terraced spa garden. The subtle, transparent symmetry of the bathtub and curved shower enclosure frames the portal to the patio creating an exterior extension of the room. Courtesy of Galina Coada.

The delicate sparkle of the wall covering and the visually stimulating vertical shower tile provide liveliness and character to this spacious bathroom. Floating vanities contribute to the lightness of the space while providing a solid base of deep, rich tones. This project was collaboration with the interior design firm Smith Stuart Interiors. Courtesy of Galina Coada.

Turn-of-the-Century Barn

A client's vision of a scaled replica of a turn-of-the-century barn in Georgia was the driving force of this home. It sits in view of horse pasture in Serenbe, an environmental community twenty miles from Atlanta. Moon Bros., Inc., architects carefully crafted this stunning home that reflects its connection with the Old South from more than 100 years ago. Courtesy of Galina Coada.

Light filters through the Douglas fir beams spanning the entire space. The natural wood and steel connections add texture and interest. The textural marble floors throughout provide a warm durable base. Courtesy of Galina Coada.

The complex structure spans forty-eight feet in both directions. True timber construction with beautiful lines and simplicity combined with dazzling geometry provide visual delight for inhabitants. Courtesy of Galina Coada.

Hand-crafted furniture grade cabinetry defines the kitchen within the open plan. Moon Bros., Inc., architects and Smith Hanes Interiors have found a perfect blend of architecture and interior design. Courtesy of Galina Coada.

The stone floor from the interior flows through the connecting breezeway and into the adjoining screened area. Textural interplay continues on the exterior with bluestone gravel offering an interesting counterpoint while also functioning as part of a rainwater control system with a hidden pipe system. As a result, Moon Bros., Inc., could fulfill the client's request to eliminate the gutters. Courtesy of Galina Coada.

The sense of simplicity and clean definitive lines continue to be reinforced in the pool area, as is the use of texture and forms. Courtesy of Galina Coada.

Timber Frame Retreat

Moon Bros., Inc., set the location of this house on a ridge to take full advantage of the spectacular views. A helicopter ride with the architect Karl de Santos and the client investigated all the possible locations and set the alignment of the home. Access to all the patios, infinity pool, and gardens is incorporated from the entire home. The timber frame retreat connects with the outdoors through vast expanses of glass. Stone columns, chimneys, and patios provide a strong base for the home and a consistent textural counterpoint to the wood. Courtesy of Galina Coada.

A stone wood-burning fireplace makes a powerful statement in a finely detailed lodge-type living area. Moon Bros., Inc., architects worked closely with William Stewart Designs throughout the house. The arched window muntins reflect the truss design. Courtesy of Galina Coada.

Douglas fir trusses, fabricated on site, span thirty-six feet to help create a stunning space with views for miles around. Tongue and groove ceilings continue from interior to exterior, enhancing the connection to the outdoors. The lighting system by Yaacov Golan of Atlanta's C Lighting is carefully integrated into the truss system. Courtesy of Galina Coada.

The kitchen serves as a central gathering space for small and large groups. The fir beams from the main living room make a smaller, more intimate statement, as does the intricate lighting. The rustic stone floors, fireplaces and arches are also continued and add cozy warmth to the room. Courtesy of Galina Coada.

Moon Bros., Inc., and William Stewart Designs wanted to make a more intimate recreation space. Warm cedar walls and ceilings, highlighted by lighting create a cozy place to gather. Natural wood floors and cabinets add subtle contrast, while maintaining the warm environment. Courtesy of Galina Coada.

What a view! This could be said of the entire house, but nowhere as much as this room. The common theme of connection to the outdoors, stone, wood, and arches are continued here. Courtesy of Galina Coada.

SHAWN O'BRIEN INTERIORS

NEW ORLEANS, LOUISIANA

My first foray into interior design was back when I was about six, and my parents let me have a say in choosing my bedroom wallpaper. I remember it like it was yesterday: pink and black line drawings of a dozen different little ballerinas, some tall and graceful, some short and squat, some pretty, and one who was puny and downright homely. I loved waking up to that wacky paper every morning. It brought a smile to my face day after day, and it also taught me an important life lesson: loving where you live is a wonderful way to begin your morning and close out your day.

Decades later, I have scads of professional design projects under my belt. Some are silly and some are serious. Some are calm, elegant, and quietly restrained, and others are colorful and edgy, vibrant and fun. Every job is entirely different from the last, but my goal is always the same: to create comfortable, beautiful, happy spaces that bring smiles to my clients' faces day after day. My philosophy is simple: people deserve to love where they live. I work really hard to make that happen, and I never forget what a privilege it is when people allow me to do it. My clients know I feel that way, and it's made for many a blissful collaboration.

701 Webster St. | New Orleans, LA 70118
504-899-3282 | www.shawnobrieninteriors.com

Art-filled Bachelor Pad Becomes Home for Newlyweds

Shawn O'Brien carried white walls throughout the living areas showcasing a decades-in-the-making art collection. In this room, she used the mint green from the Raoul linen curtains on the ceiling for an unexpected touch of color. Courtesy of Mike Terranova Photography.

The 14-foot ceilings in this eighteenth century Garden District home and white walls provided an art-gallery-like background for this colorful collection of paintings, hand-crafted furniture, sculpture, and Italian glass lighting from CX Designs. Courtesy of Mike Terranova Photography.

The broken aqua glass backsplash is the star of the kitchen. White painted cabinets, a snow-white quartz counter, Italian glass lighting from CX Designs, and a dark and shiny dining table from Julian Chichester surround it. Courtesy of Mike Terranova Photography.

A massive ebony and gilt bed from Maxine Snider, upholstered in aqua velvet, provides a restful retreat from a houseful of colorful art. Courtesy of Mike Terranova Photography.

A chunky glass sink mounted on a aqua-washed wood countertop continues the watery shades found throughout the house. Courtesy of Mike Terranova Photography.

Yet another example of watery shades of blue and green, this time in a sexy see-through bathtub adorned by a plexiglass wall sculpture. Courtesy of Mike Terranova Photography.

In collaboration with New Orleans lighting specialist Julie Neill, Shawn designed and fabricated mirrors to make a statement atop a long expanse of white marble. Dramatic nickel sconces from Vaughan Lighting complete the look. Courtesy of Mike Terranova Photography.

Master Suite in Century-Old Home

Shawn O'Brien paired marble and glass tile with a deep soaking tub, a soothing watery blue on the walls, and lush taffeta window treatments make for a luxurious bathroom retreat. Courtesy of Mike Terranova Photography.

The owner carved out a special niche for this mirrored dressing table, topped by a lush taffeta London shade, giving her a glamorous place to start the day. Courtesy of Mike Terranova Photography.

Even the water closet room, with its charming round window topped by a lush taffeta London shade, feels decked to the nines. Courtesy of Mike Terranova Photography.

The deep soaking tub looks out on a yard that provides a sea of green. Full taffeta curtains banded in watery blue and a slipcovered linen chair complete the look. Courtesy of Mike Terranova Photography.

This master suite addition to a century old house in uptown New Orleans gave the owners just the luxurious space they were looking for. Silk shades on the window, a custom oversized velvet headboard, and comfortable seating, all in soothing shades of robin's egg blue, created a delicious upstairs getaway. Courtesy of Mike Terranova Photography.

Here a furry-covered cushion on the window seat next to a deep wingchair and ottoman in a soft cut velvet make for a cozy, inviting place to curl up with a good book. Courtesy of Mike Terranova Photography.

Whimsical touches like the "Trash Day" wallpaper from Studio Printworks, red gingham shade, and red appliances turned what could be a humdrum room into a charming space. Courtesy of Mike Terranova Photography.

MASTER SUITE IN CENTURY-OLD HOME

Turn-of-the-Century Cottage Renovation

An all-time favorite iconic palm fabric made famous by the Beverly Hills Hotel; chunky 5 cm Carrera marble counters; an island created by the carpenters using salvaged wood from the demolition upstairs; a squishy sofa covered in yummy aqua chenille—the kitchen renovation satisfied everything on Shawn's checklist. Courtesy of Mike Terranova Photography.

Katrina battered this turn-of-the-century New Orleans cottage, and Shawn O'Brien brought it back to life. The living room is a happy cacophony of years of art finds, comfy furniture to sink down into with a good book, and a glorious blend of buttery yellow with tan and aqua. Courtesy of Mike Terranova Photography.

The dining room blends vibrant, hand silk screened curtain fabric from Raoul Textiles with antique Italian painted chairs, a Dutch marquetry china cabinet, and a bargain dining table find from Indonesia—a classic example of how Shawn mixes the old and the new, the precious with the common.
Courtesy of Mike Terranova Photography.

An attic bedroom destroyed when the roof failed during Hurricane Katrina became a soothing all-white retreat at day's end. The dog likes it, too... Courtesy of Mike Terranova Photography.

Oodles and oodles of Carrera tile in various shapes and sizes make for a luxurious but edgy master bath flooded with natural light. Serenades by the bells tolling from a nearby church make bath time a dream. Courtesy of Mike Terranova Photography.

Audrey, the blue Weimaraner, matches the Italian mosaic tile tub apron perfectly. Courtesy of Mike Terranova Photography.

TURN-OF-THE-CENTURY COTTAGE RENOVATION

GUY PETERSON | OFFICE OF ARCHITECTURE

SARASOTA, FLORIDA

Guy Peterson | Office for Architecture's (OFA) design studio is a studio-based practice with a team of professionals all committed to excellence in architecture and personal service to their clients. The firm's founder and principal, Guy W. Peterson, FAIA, is in his thirty-second year of private practice and has received nearly seventy design awards and honors for his work, including forty-six design awards from the American Institute of Architects. The high quality and originality of his work over an extended period of time have raised public awareness of the value of an architecture based upon honesty and simplicity. The springboard for his work has been the regional modernism of the "Sarasota School of Architecture," a recognized movement in architecture, which spanned from 1941 to 1966. The "Sarasota School" blended the cultural, vernacular, and tropical influences of traditional South Florida architecture with the philosophies of the Bauhaus. Through his use of color, indigenous materials, light and shadow, Guy Peterson has derived a softened Bauhaus aesthetic, which results in a clear, sustainable, and delightful architecture. He achieves this delight by orchestrating a sequencing of spaces that hold one's interest through a process of discovery. His commitment to advancing the cause and public value of architecture comes from a long standing belief in "essentialism, a concept which demands design by analysis and reduction rather than by stylistic imitation and embellishment."

The practice of architecture is a privilege and opportunity that Guy Peterson | OFA pursues with sensitivity through the use of sustainable design concepts both for the buildings and the landscape. Its goal is to create an architecture that will have a wide relevance and influence with the architectural culture of our society and will have lasting effects on the built environment and the quality of life.

1234 First Street | Sarasota, FL 34236
941-952-1111 | www.guypeterson.com

Frame House

West facade showing entry sequence, pool terrace, and architectural frames. Photo © Greg Wilson 2013.

The guest arrival court has views of the reflecting pool and floating walkway to entry arrival. Photo © Greg Wilson 2013.

Front entry arrival with overhead lookout and floating ipe wood mass. This view also shows the transparency of the house and floating switchback stair.
Photo © Greg Wilson 2013.

Designed by Guy Peterson, the residence has the front entry lookout showing view to the Gulf of Mexico, pool terrace, and glass floor light wells from second floor.
Photo © Greg Wilson 2013.

Second floor outdoor living room with architectural frames, glass floor, and ipe wood wall. View to the Gulf of Mexico.
Photo © Greg Wilson 2013.

Second floor outdoor living room at sunset. Photo © Greg Wilson 2013.

Second floor arrival hall showing entry to the study and transparency of the house with Gulf to Bay views. Photo © Greg Wilson 2013.

East facade showing architectural massing and floating ipe wood wall. Photo © Greg Wilson 2013.

Master bedroom entry and headboard. Views to the Gulf of Mexico. Photo © Greg Wilson 2013.

Hawthorne Street House

Entry drive and guest parking court showing layering of architectural walls and landscape elements. Photo © Greg Wilson 2013.

North facade showing guest entry sequence and landscape plinths with relation to street and sidewalk. Photo © Greg Wilson 2013.

Entry/arrival court with reflecting pool and sculptures with views inside the entry hall and to the pool beyond. Photo © Greg Wilson 2013.

North facade showing guest arrival sequence from the street. Photo © Greg Wilson 2013.

Guy Peterson's design has the dining room looking out towards the recent pool pavilion addition. Photo © Greg Wilson 2013.

The stacked block, light slivers in block, and floating roof mass in the pool pavilion relate to the existing architecture of the house. Photo © Greg Wilson 2013.

L. CRAIG ROBERTS

MOBILE, ALABAMA

A graduate of Auburn University School of Architecture, I have been a registered architect since 1979. I have practiced architecture in Mobile, Alabama, for over thirty years and have completed over one hundred-forty residential projects along the Gulf Coast area. I have designed homes that range from contemporary waterfront to elaborate traditional style mansions.

I view and practice architecture as an art form. I also design each project by incorporating my client's needs and desires and transforming them into a unique residence representing their dreams. I do this by working with my clients through the design, technical drawing, specification, and construction phases to assure they receive my total and personal attention.

My designs, which can have over thirty pages of construction drawings, can take several months to complete. My practice, albeit smaller than large firms, consists of designing two to three homes annually. This way I can diligently work for my clients and discuss their wants and needs for their homes, leading them through the sometimes daunting process of design and construction.

146 Westfield Ave. | Mobile, Al 36608
251-343-8165 | lcraigroberts@aol.com | www.l.craigroberts.com

Classic Revival

Nestled on three and one half acres on the County Club of Mobile's rolling golf course, this Classic Revival home designed by L. Craig Roberts is placed on the property so to take advantage of the views of the course that extend almost a mile to the east. With the feel of a European country estate, the grounds feature some of Mobile's most beautiful heritage live oaks. The classical interiors feature large rooms, five masonry fireplaces, and ornate ironwork throughout. Also found throughout the house are surfaces of exquisite limestone, granite, and marble.

Elegant symmetry defines the classic style home. "Old World" stucco with limestone appointments, copper adornments, slate roof, and stately chimney pots give the house an everlasting design appeal.

The rear of the home, which has views of the Mobile Country Club golf course from its eighty-foot loggia, defines this elevation.

Nestled to the kitchen side of the rear of the home is a cozy courtyard. It's a perfect place for romantic afternoon teas and dinners.

A grand classic revival home deserves a remarkable classical foyer with an impressive staircase. The owner and the architect embellished this staircase with custom designed handrails of cast iron with gold leafing.

Located alongside the kitchen, this space serves as an informal family room for relaxed meals and gatherings for the owners and family.

What splendid estate is not complete without a gentleman's room, now often referred to as a "man cave." Leather upholstered furniture, built-in bar, built-in television, and pool table offer the gentlemen a place to gather for football games and after dinner cocktails.

The great room with its 22-foot ceilings, grand fireplace, and balconies overhanging two sides, serve as an elegant gathering space for large functions. The French doors along the rear elevation give a breathtaking view of the golf course.

French Colonial / Greek Revival

This lovely cottage designed by L. Craig Roberts sits among giant oaks on the original property of one of Mobile's most historic antebellum homes, the Bragg/Mitchell House. The style is typical Greek revival with its equally spaced columns along the full length of the front elevation. Instead of a Greek revival front gable, however, a full hipped roof lends itself to the French Colonial era. Typical of many homes of the period, this home sits closer to grade than those in the low country nearer to the coast. The front steps are masonry rather than wood.

The sides of the home each have an appendage flanked with repeating French doors with fanlight transoms. On this side, you see a lovely fountain and fishpond, which produce a courtyard effect nestled against the breakfast room.

The front porch is lavish with architectural details. Notice the decorative exposed beam ceiling, window caps, diagonal board hinged shutters, and herringbone brick floor.

An interior courtyard..

French Colonial / Greek Revival

The foyer is styled after Old South country homes with a front-to-back hall called a "dog trot." Here the "dog trot" ends with an interior courtyard opened through the roof and protected by a full opening skylight.

With back-to-back fireplaces, the dining room connects to the living room with large French doors as found in homes of this historical style.

French Colonial

With its authentic brick exterior, ridge tiles, gallery porches, hipped roofline, and livable interiors, this house designed by L. Craig Roberts captures the essence of French Colonial architecture. The 3,000 square-foot house, with an additional 1,000 square feet of covered patio, is designed in perfect symmetry around a central great room. French doors access the side porches and the private courtyards, complete with unique water sculptures. The house is a reflection of what should be considered indigenous Gulf Coast Architecture with a contemporary flair and floor plan.

Today's homeowner prefers large informal spaces rather than smaller separate formal spaces. This home's primary design feature is the large great room, which serves as kitchen, dining room, and living room. Warm colors, "Old World" materials, and a wood-burning fireplace give the room its comfortable ambiance.

The home features courtyards on three sides. Two are similar, with the east and west courtyards having water fountains. Shown here on the east side of the home is a "birdbath" fountain.

In typical French Colonial style, porches surround the home on three sides. The west and east porches are lined with 8- foot tall French doors and tall thin cast iron columns, which are typical in "Old Mobile." For shade, canvas drops are between the columns.

Identical master baths flank each side of the master bedroom. Featuring a custom vanity with a basin sink on Alabama marble atop four cast iron newel posts, the entire design pulled the wall forward to offer a deep custom medicine cabinet with a framed mirror.

Italianate "New" Old Home

Snuggled in the charming confines of Old Spring Hill in Mobile, Alabama, this Italianate "new" old home is L. Craig Robert's modern representation of one of Mobile's historic downtown mansions. The brick veneer, windows, roof cornices, and porches use the same design and authentic material as found in the original home.

Popular along the northern Gulf Coast between 1855 and 1890, the Italianate style is typified by large bracketed cornices, brick or stucco exterior walls, tall vertical windows, often with embellished eyebrow tops, and a lacy iron porch.

ITALIANATE "NEW" OLD HOME

Interior rooms show off the large vertical windows. Typical also in period homes from this era are heart pine floors.

This is a lovely example of a period-appropriate oversized column type newel post made from heart of pine. Note, the ceramic tile foyer floor, which is a typical feature of this style.

A view of the rear yard and a period cast iron fountain can be seen through the vertical windows of the breakfast room and rear porch.

studioWTA

NEW ORLEANS, LOUISIANA

In studioWTA's downtown New Orleans converted warehouse space, the pervasive spatial experience is one of openness and creativity. This expression is a direct manifestation of our firm philosophy: an open, collaborative, and integrated team approach, including everyone in our studio, our partnering consultants, and, especially, our clients, focusing on the craft of architecture conveyed through its details. From small interior renovations and installations to large multi-family adaptive reuse and planning schemes, we attempt to establish a dialogue between the idealized and the idiosyncratic by recognizing and focusing on the visual and spatial connections between building and context, program and user, technology and aesthetics to address new questions of program, environment, change, movement, and expression. Through commitment to a shared ideal, the diverse talents of individual artists, contractors, craftsmen, and people who utilize a space are given expression and value.

1119 Tchoupitoulas St. | New Orleans, LA 70130
504-593-9074 | www.studiowta.com

Rice Mill Lofts

On a sweeping curve of the Mississippi River in New Orleans, studioWTA's adaptive reuse of an historic masonry and heavy timber warehouse brings a fresh, modern interpretation of loft living to one of the city's most vibrant neighborhoods, with a focus on communal space, open living, and connection to the arts. Historic brick and plaster are restored at both interior and exterior locations, and existing graffiti is preserved in place as a nod to the previous occupation of the building by traveling artists and musicians. Courtesy of seanc@ekisticsinc.net.

RICE MILL LOFTS

The main entrance, on a restored cobbled street, is marked by generous glazing, projecting overhang and door pulls designed and fabricated by a local craftsman. Courtesy of Neil Alexander.

Spacious common corridors on the upper floors focus on the view toward the Mississippi River and downtown New Orleans, and provide varied opportunities for resident interaction and social gatherings. Courtesy of Neil Alexander.

Throughout the building in both common corridors and individual residences, existing graffiti is maintained as part of the building's story. Heavy timber columns and beams reveal themselves and play off the smooth surfaces of new walls and lush, textured flooring to highlight the juxtaposition of historic and modern architecture. Courtesy of seanc@ekisticsinc.net.

First floor live/work units take advantage of high ceilings to incorporate a bedroom loft above the core kitchen/bath/utility insertion. Polished concrete floors, heavy timber columns, and minimal kitchens reinforce the industrial aesthetic of the space. Courtesy of seanc@ekisticsinc.net.

Overlooking the river, townhouse residences are located along the rear of the building. Lofted master bedroom suites here are enhanced by the exposed historic roof structure restored in place that include original steel connections. Courtesy of Neil Alexander.

Whimsical light fixtures, varied textures and exposed historic structural elements combine in the common areas to reinforce the lofts' industrial aesthetic and invite residents to occupy the corridors at various locations. Courtesy of seanc@ekisticsinc.net.

Roof monitor windows on the river side of the building correspond to the two-story townhouses, bringing in natural light and views to the lofted master bedroom suites. Courtesy of Neil Alexander.

A rooftop terrace, complete with several large gathering areas and covered spaces, takes advantage of the building's siting along a prominent curve of the Mississippi River to allow expansive and sweeping views of downtown New Orleans. Residents frequently gather here for cocktails or dinners as a community. Courtesy of Neil Alexander.

The communal pool is situated between the building and the river levee wall, complete with statuary and lush landscaping. The large vertical opening in the building reveals common corridors on each floor and gives the shared spaces of the building a visual connection to the neighborhood and the city. Courtesy of Neil Alexander.

RICE MILL LOFTS

A Pair of Two-Story Volumes

Interpreting the historic vernacular of New Orleans homes, this residence designed by studioWTA is arranged as a pair of two-story volumes connected by a recessed, double-height living space overlooking a lush pool and garden. At twilight, the illumination of the recess highlights the polycarbonate wall at the second floor, marking the entrance through the private front court. Plaster and cement board cladding break down the massing and bring a residential scale to the house. Tucked into one corner of the ground floor, the owner's private practice office is accessible to clients through the courtyard and a dedicated entrance, separated from the living area of the residence. Courtesy of Jeffrey Johnston.

The soaring double height living space at the center of the house is a connective joint between the stacked areas on both sides, overlooked by the open kitchen, second floor walkway, and spiral stair to the roof terrace. Courtesy of Neil Alexander.

The exterior finishes give the house a modern, dynamic motion. The corner window in the office frames a view toward a nearby church. Courtesy of Wayne Troyer.

The cement board cladding attachment system is carefully and deliberately executed, giving the house a machined quality that is then softened by texture and composition of the massing elements. Courtesy of Wayne Troyer.

A PAIR OF TWO-STORY VOLUMES

The dramatic steel-framed opening at the double height living room breaks open the corner of the house and invites the garden inside, blurring the line between the two and enhancing the experience. Courtesy of Jeffrey Johnston.

The owners were invested in an open plan for their master bedroom suite, including their bathroom. Space flows freely between the bedroom and bathroom, with the freestanding shower and vanity acting to shield the suite from the more public areas of the house. Courtesy of Neil Alexander.

The recessed courtyard breaks down the mass of the house along the street, allowing the modern structure to be elegantly inserted into the existing fabric. The dramatic view of the courtyard at twilight highlights the layering of materials, texture, mass, and openings experienced upon approach from the street. Courtesy of Neil Alexander.

City Park Avenue Residence

In a gracious home overlooking New Orleans' City Park, a family modernized their interior to complement their lifestyle and showcase their considerable modern art and furniture collection. At the rear of the house and just off the kitchen, studioWTA designed a new wood and glass addition to overlook the garden. It frames views down the street lined with live oaks and provides an informal dining area for the owners. The steps down into the backyard access a detached garage and landscaped areas. Courtesy of Sara Essex Bradley.

The new addition is accessed from the back garden via a stair framed on one side with an armature for growing vines. The expanse of glass in the wall is protected from heat gain by the trellis extension and the rich wood is complimented by the copper accents of the gutter and downspout. Courtesy of Sara Essex Bradley.

The fully renovated and modernized kitchen features custom designed and fabricated bamboo cabinets and quartz countertops and ebonized metallic floor tiles. The overall effect is of a sophisticated but accessible area for cooking, gathering, and dining. The view of the oak trees through the breakfast room adjacent pull the greenery and natural light of the outside into one of the most used spaces of the house. Courtesy of Sara Essex Bradley.

Across from the kitchen island, an existing masonry chimney has been left in place with new custom cabinetry designed around it to feature the owners' serving ware and cookbooks. The exaggerated recess of the base gives the cabinets the sense of floating. Cork wall tiles provide a place to pin up photos or notes. Courtesy of Sara Essex Bradley.

The small butler's pantry bar located adjacent to the kitchen picks up on the design of that space, with custom cabinetry, display area, and variegated tile backsplash. Courtesy of Sara Essex Bradley.

A translucent sliding panel door brings shared natural light from the bedroom into the second floor hallway and creates a sense of spatial continuity. Modern aluminum and wood detailing of the door frame and casing contrasts with the traditional wood baseboard of the hallway, reinforcing studioWTA's design intention to integrate new and old sensitively. Courtesy of Sara Essex Bradley.

At the end of the second floor hallway is "His" bath. The same translucent, sliding panel door strategy is put to use in a dramatic floor-to-ceiling application to conceal the bathroom and bring shared natural light into the hallway. The juxtaposition of the panel adjacent to the existing masonry chimney and the reclaimed wood floor creates elegant textural shifts. The master bedroom door can be seen to the right and a den to the left. The hallway is opened up to create a gallery space for a large portion of the owner's art collection, turning what is typically an interstitial space into an important moment in the house in its own right. Courtesy of Sara Essex Bradley.

The master bedroom is a calm, modern oasis, featuring a custom designed and fabricated wardrobe and the sliding panel opening to the hallway. Generous natural light bathes the rich, reclaimed wood floor in warmth. Courtesy of Sara Essex Bradley.

At the end of the second floor hallway, "His" bath features a custom-designed vanity, concealed storage behind mirrors, mahogany floor-to-ceiling window, and dark tiled floor. The minimal shower can be seen in the mirror. A single glass pane provides the enclosure; the floor-to-ceiling tile emphasizes the height of the room. Courtesy of Sara Essex Bradley.

In "Her" bath, light colors, textures, and fixtures add a calmness and softness to the space and emphasize the spaciousness of the room, which features a freestanding sculptural bathtub, walk-in shower, and custom-designed vanity table. The alignment of the soaking tub with the quartz-framed window and pendant light fixture reinforces the tub as the centerpiece and allows views of the city park across the street while soaking. Courtesy of Sara Essex Bradley.

THOMAS & DENZINGER ARCHITECTS

CHARLESTON, SOUTH CAROLINA

We consider the making of architecture to be a creative response to the land. The land comes first and, when our work is done, one should be able to feel how the features of the site inspired the form of the buildings and gardens. The structure itself we understand to be but a part of a larger identity. Trees, dunes, marshes, the sea, breezes, smells, history, sky, the sun, and the moon are all elements of the greater composition. We recognize that a deceptive modesty of the building's structure can often achieve a higher level of elegance in the way structure orchestrates the way man interacts with nature. The success of a design can be judged by the extent to which the design reveals the sense of place, to which it articulates that connection between place and human identity.

Thomas & Denzinger is known for the creativity of our architecture, for the highly individualistic response of each of our selective projects to the specific site, and to the spiritual considerations, as well as to the physical needs, of our clients.

51 Elizabeth St. | Charleston, SC 29403
843-723-6651. | www.thomasanddenzinger.com

Elevated Oasis

The ocean, horizon, and sky can be seen through the light steel gates at the central passage. Hidden garage bays to the left and right are positioned below living spaces with the pool and garden above serving as a private outdoor space and enhancing the flanking living spaces. Photo © Greg Wilson 2013.

A glorious welcome—the site, home, and landscape extend an invitation. The Thomas & Denzinger residence flows as a series of indoor/outdoor spaces, always relating back to the water and intensifying the awareness of the natural surroundings and the lifestyle of those within. Photo © Greg Wilson 2013.

Upon entry to the grade level realm, a slightly raised ipe boardwalk extends below pool windows. The windows allow light and shadow to penetrate and reiterate the importance of the water in its connectivity of house and site. Photo © Greg Wilson 2013.

ELEVATED OASIS

Stop. Look up. Take in the wonder from above, then proceed up the main stair to experience the water, garden, and ocean in a different way from the pool deck. Photo © Greg Wilson 2013.

Natural forms prevalent on the island and in the sea inspire the oval stair. Looking down from the third level kitchen deck, one catches a glimpse of the pool deck and garden. Photo © Greg Wilson 2013.

Three main interior spaces—dining, living, and entry vestibule—are captured here as conceived by Thomas & Denzinger Architects. The dining area, half a level above the living and entry spaces, provides a formal dining space while it maintains openness and captures views to the ocean and pool garden. Custom mahogany windows and doors follow the contours of the roof plane, maximizing natural light and enhancing the graceful swoop of the form. Lift and slide doors open to the pool deck, allowing not only a seamless visual integration of spaces but a physical one as well. Photo © Greg Wilson 2013.

At dusk, the pool, surrounding vegetation, and house vibrantly reflect the mood of the Gulf of Mexico as the sun sets radiantly to the West.

The axial pool creates a connection between the Charlotte Sound to the East and Gulf of Mexico to the West. An ipe pool deck meets a coquina surround and raised garden at a level above the ground. The water, rippling over glass pool tile, appears to overflow into the Gulf beyond. Photo © Greg Wilson 2013.

The passage below the pool offers a direct connection aboard a slightly raised ipe deck to the colony of sea grapes, beach, and ocean. Concrete columns support a pool and deck system above. Windows in the bottom of the pool let light into the passage, which reiterates the importance of the water in its connectivity of house and site. Photo © Greg Wilson 2013.

From the sandy white beach—after arriving through a grove of sea grapes, saline grasses, and resilient palms—one looks back to see the form of the house, inspired by ocean waves, simultaneously welcoming and protecting. Photo © Greg Wilson 2013.

Filtered light through the cedar lattice and the filigree of palm fronds extends a gracious welcome to residents and visitors arriving at the Elevated Oasis. Photo © Greg Wilson 2013.

A custom spiral stair leads from grade level to the pool deck. Stringers are constructed of laminated and painted wood. A stainless steel frame enables ipe treads to float between stringers, while a stainless steel and ipe rail winds to the level above. Photo © Greg Wilson 2013.

Maritime Forces

The double story trellis at the pool deck articulates the continuation of a double height gallery that runs through the house and site. The trellis provides shade from the high and unrelenting southern summer sun while allowing low sunlight to enter the house in cooler winter months. Photo © William Struhs.

At the base of the structure, an oyster shell aggregate masonry is overlaid with wooden lattice supporting a network of vines, integrating the structure with the maritime forest. The undulating roof is separated from the walls vertically by a system of louvered panels. Suggesting a sense of breathing, the louvers articulate light, air, and privacy. Photo © William Struhs.

Through layering the oyster shell aggregate masonry chimneys, a series of louvers, and an applied wood lattice covered with vegetation, Thomas & Denzinger Architects created a fully integrated structure. Photo © William Struhs.

Undulating roof forms reflect the rhythmic wave action of the ocean. A linear trellis defines entry to both the main and guest houses. Inside the main house, this trellis is articulated in a double story gallery and emerges again along the pool as a passage to the ocean. Photo © William Struhs.

The play of light along the site's central spine reflects off the masonry walls and bluestone ground cover. The bluestone marches inside the entrance of the main house and out to the pool deck beyond, creating a continuity and flow from outside to inside and back out again. Photo © William Struhs.

Inside the central atrium, the bluestone floor delineates a sense of passage, strengthened by linear natural light from above. The second level gallery is open to below but maintains a sense of privacy through the wooden louvers at balcony level. A glass bridge on the second level floats above the entry. Photo © William Struhs.

Here the trellis emerges again as a passage toward the ocean reveals itself. A neutral color palate finds harmony with the surrounding site. Photo © William Struhs.

Living and dining areas grow off of the central spine, setting up museum-like spaces for the owner's collection of fine art. The result is a place in which living is enhanced by design—that of the structure and art within and that of the surrounding natural environment. Photo © William Struhs.

A masonry fireplace anchors the living room. Important pieces of the owner's art collection are highlighted on either side. The warm heart pine floors of the living room meet the bluestone passage at a seamless transition and the room opens to the pool deck to the south. Photo © William Struhs.

Ah, isn't this the way we all should live? Photo © William Struhs.

Looking down from the glass and steel bridging the entry, clean lines, materials, textures, color, and light integrate into a rich composition. Photo © William Struhs.

Shifting Planes

From the marsh at dusk, a gravel path leads the way to a glowing charge of light radiating from inside. A dark cedar tower contrasts with the raw concrete and bleached cedar shakes of the facades. Photo © William Struhs.

Twelve shifting planes of concrete align to establish a framework for the structure designed by Thomas & Denzinger Architects. The main entrance sequence from a granite and gravel drive, up the bluestone steps flanked with bamboo, through a wall of steel, glass, and cedar shakes offers a warm welcome, set between parallel walls of concrete. Photo © William Struhs.

A double story gallery runs the length of the house—a stair terminating one end and a wall of glass the other. Thin steel window frames slip between heavy steel columns to the south, and a mezzanine leads to second level living and bedroom spaces to the north. The tower room is accessed via an upper set of stairs and across a glass bridge to the east. Photo © William Struhs.

The living room opens to the tidal wetlands. All materials in the house come together here, and the sensitivity to placement of structure in the site fully discloses its vitality. Photo © William Struhs.

A node at the core of the living room, outdoor porch, and pool deck, this 16 cubic-foot screened cube embodies outdoor living in coastal South Carolina. A big fan keeps air flowing in the sultry summer months, and a wood-burning stove provides warmth on a rare but chilly winter day. Photo © William Struhs.

Kitchen and living spaces flow together, and openings in the parallel concrete walls align to reveal the wet bar and dining room. Flanked with brown truffle SieMatic cabinetry to the left and a custom steel fireplace to the right, an asymmetrical but balanced composition and material palate define the home's makeup and sensibility. Photo © William Struhs.

The invisible edge of the pool appears to fall into the marsh beyond. The light and color of the marsh and river influence the mood of the pool itself. Photo © William Struhs.

SHIFTING PLANES

The glassy reflection of the pool mirrors the intimate nature of the site and reflects its ever-changing mood through season and light. Photo © William Struhs.

Harmony, continuity, and grace fill the spaces between shifting planes of concrete. An indoor/outdoor steel, glass, and ipe stairwell connects the main house (on the right) to the guesthouse (on the left) and offers a glimpse of the marsh and river beyond. Photo © William Struhs.

Rhythm. Composition. Integration with natural surroundings. Darkness and light. Privacy and embrace. These elements entrust the residence and the occupants with depth of experience and excitement. Photo © William Struhs.

TONIC DESIGN | TONIC CONSTRUCTION

RALEIGH, NORTH CAROLINA

Through our two separate yet interacting companies, Tonic Design and Tonic Construction, we design and build sensitive, modern architectural solutions that make a difference in our clients' lives, enhance the existing architectural fabric of our projects' communities, and contribute to environmental sustainability.

As a design/build firm, we bring hands-on knowledge of both design and construction to every project, whether we're serving solely as architect, solely as general contractor, or, in the best-case scenarios, as both.

The influence of construction on design and design on construction shapes our process and defines our approach to architecture. That's why we prefer to call what we do "construction-led design" rather than "design/build." We thoroughly enjoy the craftsmanship of building, and we're just as proud of what we build as we are of what we design.

Through our building experience, we've also gained solid relationships with consultants and craftspeople whose knowledge and talents are perfectly aligned with our designs. These professionals help us determine the feasibility of any design or construction concept quickly, without wasting time and materials. They also play an integral part in the process of our work and as valuable "editors." With their help, we are constantly aware of what can be designed and built for a specific place or price. We also know that what we design we can, in fact, build—sometimes despite conventional wisdom!

As architect and builder, we begin a design project keenly aware of the costs, the skill levels of subcontractors, regional market fluctuations, and available technologies. Working with a construction expert and design professional at the same time ensures that potential problems are discovered before the project starts.

209 Bickett Blvd. | Raleigh, NC 278608
919-803-4278 | vincent@tonic-design.com | www.tonic-design.com

Modernism Meets Regionalism

The clients bought the five-acre property, with the intention of building a simple, modern home in a clearing amidst a lush forest. They wanted the house to disturb the natural environment as little as possible and accommodate local wildlife. Tonic Design/Tonic Construction sited the house carefully to avoid disturbing the natural environment, to maximize natural lighting, and to frame views of forest, including a favorite three-trunked tree. Courtesy of Todd Lanning, Gravitation Studios.

To reflect the rural setting, Tonic Design/Tonic Construction specified simple, inexpensive materials and references to regional agricultural structures rendered in a modern architecture composition. Courtesy of Richard Leo Johnson/Atlantic Archives, Inc.

Recalling old farm sheds, the house's skewed cubic form is clad in solid and perforated COR-TEN®, a steel alloy developed to eliminate the need for painting. The steel forms a stable rust-like appearance when exposed to the weather. As a result, the house will be a constantly evolving element in the landscape as a rich patina develops over the years. The COR-TEN also acts as a rain screen, canopy, sunshade, and visual screen. Courtesy of Richard Leo Johnson/Atlantic Archives, Inc.

The first floor includes the entry, a spacious kitchen/living/dining room, a studio/music space, and two decks. The second floor includes the master bedroom suite and two bedrooms for the children, who share extra loft space and bath. The perforated metal reappears inside as a stair railing. Space under the stairs is a cozy play area for the children. Courtesy of Richard Leo Johnson/Atlantic Archives, Inc.

Tonic Construction completed the home for $155 per square foot, thanks in large part to the design/build process and the readily available materials, including oak. Spray foam insulation, tightly sealed ducts, low-e glazed windows, and Energy Star® appliances contribute to the home's energy conservation. Although their new house is 800 feet larger than their previous house, the owners report that their energy bills are, on average, 30 percent lower. Courtesy of Richard Leo Johnson/Atlantic Archives, Inc.

As for stewardship of the natural wildlife, the National Wildlife Federation recently certified the property as a natural habitat. Courtesy of Richard Leo Johnson/Atlantic Archives, Inc.

As Green As You Can Get

At the end of each bar, overhangs with photovoltaic panels provide shading as well as solar energy. The central space where the three bars meet, with a highest point of 22 feet, has a kitchen, dining, and living spaces and is open to the second story and continuous balcony above. Visual connections are the essence of the house, which boasts a combination of storefront floor-to-ceiling and aluminum-framed operable and non-operable windows.
Courtesy of Todd Lanning, Gravitation Studios.

Maple built-ins and cabinets designed by Tonic Design line many of the rooms. Floors are maple as well, and decks outside are ipe wood. The house effectively captures natural light in every room, and careful placement of electrical lighting both inside and out creates a warm feel enhanced by the sculpted ceilings and soffits.
Courtesy of Todd Lanning, Gravitation Studios.

This Tonic Design/Tonic Construction residence is composed of two primary design components: bars and panels. Each acts together to generate an environmentally sensitive response. Narrow bars composed of private space branch out into the landscape to create courtyards, capture natural light, allow cross ventilation, and intersect to form a central volume of double height public space. Exterior cladding is a mix of brick veneer, zinc, and vertical cedar panels. Courtesy of Todd Lanning, Gravitation Studios.

ED WEBER ARCHITECTS

CHARLESTON, WEST VIRGINIA

When an architect from Chicago's Gold Coast moves to the coal mining capitol of West Virginia, you might expect his career to become as obscured as an Appalachian meadow in a summer morning's mist. However, obscurity has never been an option. I moved to Charleston in 2006 and joined the oldest architectural firm in town, building a residential niche until forming my own firm in May 2012. Working in what I call the smallest big city in America has offered opportunities to design on a wide range of projects in the public and private realm; from a large corporate headquarters, to home renovations, additions, and new construction, a riverfront amphitheater, and the historic restoration of the state supreme court's courtroom space. This rich and diverse collection of project types and styles has transformed a small residential architect from the big city into one of the region's most sought after architects.

Our success has been predicated on three factors: We put the clients' needs, values, goals, aesthetics, and budget at the center of the design process. We believe in creating healthy, durable, and energy-efficient buildings in harmony with their environment and creating a unique sense of place. We aspire to bring an innovative edge to each project that reaches beyond our clients' dreams and expectations, revealing a hidden aspect of who they are and what architecture is supposed to be.

This very personal and passionate approach leads each client on a path of discovery as the first of several design meetings, plans, sketches, and 3-D models develop into material samples and construction drawings. Soon thereafter, the building begins and what were just dreams become reality. We strive to make the process simple and fun while building both long-lasting projects and relationships.

6 Arlington Ave. | Charleston, WV 25302
304-932-8007 | www.edweberarchitects.com

Natural Beauty

This contemporary Arts and Crafts style home combines four materials; stone, wood, stucco, and metal to create a human scale composition, allowing the natural beauty of the materials to dominate while adding to the drama to be found on the other side of the entry door. Courtesy of Michael Adkins.

Entering the house, one circulates around the central fireplace and is rewarded with the soaring ceiling, treetop view, and open warmth of the hearth and home. Ed Weber Architects oriented the residence along a ridgeline to allow the great room to be washed with indirect light and beautiful vistas. Courtesy of Tracy Toliver.

Natural hickory flooring is repeated on the ceiling supported by cedar trusses, as the stair ascends from the lower level providing a dynamic connection to the lower terrace, guest room, and man-cave. Courtesy of Rick Lee.

The kitchen lets the outdoors in while communicating directly with the great and dining rooms to either side. Pocket doors close the kitchen when the cooks need their creative space private. Courtesy of Rick Lee.

The dining room is designed for group entertaining, open air comfort, and natural light. The double-vaulted ceiling helps orient the room to south and west views. Courtesy of Tracy Toliver.

The master bedroom features a romantic sunken spa within an alcove with floor to ceiling windows. It is enclosed by shoji screens. Courtesy of Tracy Toliver.

The master bathroom does not sacrifice natural light, privacy, or comfort. Courtesy of Rick Lee.

The two-story side of the house shows the left to right organization of the master bedroom, great room, kitchen, and dining room. Below the dining room is a cellar with screen walls made from the decking material where the home's 5,000-gallon rainwater cisterns can be found. Captured rainwater is converted to drinking water, one of the many green design features. Courtesy of Ed Weber.

The deck features a cantilevered boardwalk extending over the landscape where one can find a peaceful retreat and commune with the nature. Courtesy of Michael Adkins.

Ed Weber, Architect, says, "It is my belief that every work of architecture should provide a special place where the human spirit and the nature can harmonize and delight in the comfort of the eternal now. Where we collect our thoughts and connect them to the all-pervasive life force."

Art House Redux

Locally renowned architect Clint Bryan designed this 1970s quad-level home. Derived from the style of the era popularized by architects such as Charles Moore and Robert Venturi, Bryan used a series of multi-directional shed and gable roofs to the effect of colliding geometric forms. In the renovation, Ed Weber's design gutted two middle levels and added a new entry and the master bedroom suite wing to the left of main house. Weber uses forms with similar dramatic affect as Bryan to create a home for an art-collecting couple that showcases their collection. Courtesy of Tracy Toliver.

Visitors are greeted by a sculpture that compliments the new wing of the house. The house was made more accessible with the new ramp and entry and master suite on the main living level of the house. Courtesy of Tracy Toliver.

The main level was gutted, removing most walls and creating a new wide stair into the living room. Courtesy of Tracy Toliver.

The main level view towards the entry foyer expresses the intersecting vertical planes of the existing house and addition, creating visual movement and adventure. Courtesy of Tracy Toliver.

The upper level view into the living room shows the interplay of art and architecture to form a unified composition: a living room setting within a museum. Courtesy of Tracy Toliver.

The focal point of the seating area is this painting as another sculpture dances from the balcony. Courtesy of Tracy Toliver.

The new kitchen was relocated as the keystone of the home's "U-shaped" plan. Courtesy of Tracy Toliver.

The simple yet functional kitchen lets the party's favorite gathering place be the star of the show. Courtesy of Tracy Toliver.

The master bedroom is bathed in natural light from a window wall at the tall end of the room. Moonlight views and golden sunrises are a daily delight. Courtesy of Tracy Toliver.

The reverse angle of the master bathroom allows natural light, sky views, and privacy. Courtesy of Tracy Toliver.

Core Values

This historically significant property sits along the Kanawha River outside of Charleston, West Virginia, and was one of the first salt works in the region. Known as the Dickinson Salt Works, the estate has been under the ownership of one family since 1805. In addition to the main residence, the property includes a small saltbox style residence, the company store building, a concrete block garage with a small shed roof addition on the side, a large end gable barn with a partial silo and flanking shed roof wings with lofts, a modern gable, one-story, maintenance and office building, a brick cellar house/cistern with concrete pillars, a one-and-one-half story, end gable barn/garage, and a one-and-one-half story end gable tool shed. The house also has extensive gardens and pastures for raising Belted Galloway cattle. Courtesy of Tracy Toliver.

In 1925, renowned architect Walter Martens extensively renovated the main house in the Colonial Revival style. For the past 88 years, the house weathered storms, floods, termites, and the general debilitating effects of age. Several years ago, the owners found extensive damage to the structure. Rather that demolishing a family icon, they hired Ed Weber Architect to propose a cost effective solution to the structural issues as well as replace the existing electric, plumbing and HVAC systems, and insulate the exterior walls. The challenge was to renovate the core of the house from within while maintaining the aesthetic qualities of the house.

To insulate certain portions of the house, the siding was removed and insulation installed from the outside. Shutters were rebuilt and wood trim and roof repaired. Courtesy of Tracy Toliver.

Extensive termite damage can be seen. The house was deteriorating from within. Courtesy of Ed Weber.

The renovated stair hall with new wall and ceiling finishes, refinished floor, and stair treads. Courtesy of Tracy Toliver.

The living room and dining room were completely gutted and restored to the original decor. The family matriarchs can be seen over the living room fireplaces. Courtesy of Tracy Toliver.

ANDREW A. WILLETT ARCHITECT, PA

ASHEVILLE, NORTH CAROLINA

At Andrew A. Willett, Architect, we strive to find designs that blend familiar themes and iconography, but present them in a new, yet still timeless, way. Our goal is to maintain some level of the past our clients know, but at the same time reintroduce it to them with fresh new look. Beyond that, our main goal as a firm is to bring elegant solutions that capture each client's unique aesthetic. We want to ensure that their dreams—not ours—are fulfilled. We are here to create a beautiful stage for their lives to unfold upon and that of the many generations to follow. Skills coupled with a casualness and a fun factor is part of our message!

88 Church St. | Asheville, NC 28801
828-253-1001 | www.awillettarchitect.com

A Creek Flows Through It

While this house sits on quite a lovely piece of land with great views, the client opted to create an inward focused house. Andrew A. Willett created a man-made creek and a "V" shaped house to surround it.

Andrew Willett says, "The symbiotic relationship this house has to water seemed to ask us for a blend of Japanese inspired forms. Mix in some Appalachian materials, and you end up with a confluence of thought I like to call Jappalachian." Courtesy of J. Weiland Photographer.

Because of the scale of the boulders used, the process was to build the foundation, set the boulders at the perimeter and inside the house, and then build the house around them. A first-time technique for the firm! The large boulder seen in the image finds its way into the master shower eventually! Courtesy of J. Weiland Photographer.

This upper level media room gave a great opportunity to get a full 360-degree view and that "tree house feel." It also allowed for a tower element to draw your eyes to the center of this jewel. Courtesy of J. Weiland Photographer.

The firm typically likes to keep the ceilings clear of lighting. In this space, it used a flexible "S" lighting track floating below the ceiling and trusses. Courtesy of J. Weiland Photographer.

Bring Me the Sunshine

This house had a very difficult lot. It was rather narrow, yet had about 50 feet of vertical fall. After a few iterations, Andrew Willett designed a tiered garden wall system, and an "L" shaped plan that allowed for the maximum quantity of light to flow into each room. The firm used brick here with a lower pitch hip roof to keep the house visually tight to the land..."hunkered down" as they say. Courtesy of John Warner Photography.

Asheville's moderate climate beckons for a generous porch flowing out of the living room. Courtesy of John Warner Photography.

In this area of North Carolina, the use of cedar shingles above brick is common. The firm and the client opted for stucco over brick to create a new twist to this theme and to reduce the maintenance. Courtesy of John Warner Photography.

Soft wall tones blend well with the nutmeg toned cabinets, honed soapstone tops, and glass tile backsplash. Courtesy of J. Weiland Photographer.

Willett's design places kitchen islands in non-orthogonal orientations to create some visual dynamics to the space. Courtesy of J. Weiland Photographer.

Alchemy Designs designed this luxurious vanity in walnut. Courtesy of J. Weiland Photographer.

Shinto in the Hills

The original concept of this house was based on the firm's musings on Shinto shrines. Add to the program that a 25-foot x 50-foot log cabin was the heart of this structure! In the end, Andrew Willett basically encapsulated the cabin by adding wings and increasing the ceiling heights in the new spaces to accommodate the client's desires. Courtesy of J. Weiland Photographer.

The shoji screen inspired entry door. Also note the soft fiber optic lighting on the columns. Courtesy of J. Weiland Photographer.

Willett frequently creates masculine stone elements, but tapers the stone to make the appearance slightly more delicate. The mix of masculine and the feminine has proven to be the best balance. Courtesy of J. Weiland Photographer.

The firm uses tall doors with transoms above to maximize light and establishes a human scale through the modest door panels. Courtesy of J. Weiland Photographer.

With the owner's sculpture floating in front of the large picture window, the boundaries between inside and outside start to disappear. Courtesy of J. Weiland Photographer.

Mandala Design created the counters, sinks, and fireplace surround. Courtesy of J. Weiland Photographer.

The material palette here includes site-harvested walnut and sycamore, a custom, ergonomically fitted concrete tub, and the owner's art. Courtesy of J. Weiland Photographer.

Creating open space with a richly layered composition is no easy task! The shape of the island is based on a highly modified version of the "Golden Mean" or "Golden Rectangle." The perfect architectural curve, one able to be derived from simple scalable geometric terms, is the tail of the dragon that Willett has been chasing since his college thesis. He's getting closer to this deceptive beast. Courtesy of J. Weiland Photographer.

Bent Views to the Black Mountains

Here in the mountains the lay of the land has a strong voice. Frequently, Andrew Willett bends houses so they can hug the land as seen here. Courtesy of J. Weiland Photographer.

A rich yet varied material palette: exposed tapered rafter tails, heavy timber brackets, flared shingle coursing, and vertical board and baton. Also note, the nice flair kicker detailing at the window. Courtesy of J. Weiland Photographer.

The corner fireplace is back to back to the living room corner fireplace to provide some level of economy of construction. Courtesy of J. Weiland Photographer.

The firm uses transoms as a bonding element over both windows and doors to enhance a strong horizontal. Courtesy of J. Weiland Photographer.

WINN WITTMAN ARCHITECTURE

AUSTIN, TEXAS

There is a lot of sameness in contemporary architecture today—boxy designs with little inspiration and individuality. Our homes are both art-pieces of sculpture that can be appreciated from any angle and also highly functional and sustainable systems for living. We don't have a "style;" rather, our style for each project is derived from our client's essential "vibe" and their aspirations about how they would like to live. Also, we limit our practice almost exclusively to high-end contemporary homes (we also do select restaurants and stores), because that's what inspires us and that's what we are known for.

Over the past fifteen years, we have analyzed, refined, and re-scripted the various stages of designing a home. Our proprietary system, The Wittman Process®, is the culmination of our vision and experience in streamlining the process of conceiving and delivering extraordinarily unique residences.

Our home base in Austin, Texas, is known as the "live music capitol of the world," and our clients include several well-known musicians. This past year, a Hollywood film directed by Terrence Malick featured two of our homes. Although most of our clients aren't famous, we still seek to treat them all like rock stars—which is fitting, because *Spaces Magazine* called our founder, Winn Wittman AIA, "America's most rock 'n roll architect."

Our work has received recognition and awards from the American Institute of Architects, The Dream Home Awards, World Architecture News, Green Building and Design, Signature Kitchens and Baths, and others. Our projects have been featured in such magazines as *Architectural Record, The Robb Report, Luxe, Luxury Home Quarterly, Hinge, Urban Home,* and *Design Bureau*—as well as in programs on HGTV and the Discovery Channel. We are members of the American Institute of Architects and the Texas Society of Architects, and we serve clients throughout Texas and around the world.

1108 Lavaca | Suite 110-488
Austin, TX 78701 | 512-630-2724 | www.winnwittman.com

Casa de Corazon

The client said they wanted their retirement home to look like the "bones of the earth." This metaphor inspired Winn Wittman's repetitive structural supports, which are made of curved steel on the outside and laminated wood on the inside of the home (for a thermal break) and give the effect of a ribcage. The home is located off the grid on an 85-acre farm, west of Austin, Texas. This area is also prone to wildfires, so the client wanted a fire-resistant home, and a home with minimal landscaping to reduce fire risk. Courtesy of Coles Hairston.

The unique roof structure covers three volumes: the main home, the guesthouse, and the garage. The roof also channels water to a central gutter, where it is directed to an underground cistern for use during the hot Texas summers. Locals dubbed the home "case de corazon" after the heart-shaped profile of the side elevation. Courtesy of Coles Hairston.

CASA DE CORAZON

The northern orientation of all major windows, combined with soy-foam insulation in the roof and walls, ensures that the operational costs are low. The materials used, which include local limestone laid in a coursed pattern and metal roofing, reflect the local vernacular of the nineteenth and twentieth century Texas farm house, but in an updated form. Courtesy of Coles Hairston.

Soaring Wings

This home's large copper "wings" were inspired by the large birds that circle the thermals in this hilly area located ten minutes outside Austin. The home is divided into a public wing and a private wing, which are separated by a two-story glass and steel bridge. This creates greater privacy for the bedroom areas, which was needed by this family with young children. Courtesy of Coles Hairston.

A large gallery upstairs features a 40-foot curved floor-to-ceiling window, which offers unobstructed views of the hill country. Motorized mesh shades programmed to an astronomical clock raise and lower with the sun. Courtesy of Coles Hairston.

Carved into the hillside, the courtyard features a salt-water swimming/zen-like reflecting pool surrounded by bamboo. Also offering a Zen-like rock garden, it is a private refuge from the hot Texas sun. The owners believe the home is a complex, rich, and ultimately satisfying framework for their life. Courtesy of Coles Hairston.

The home is separated into a public volume, containing the living, eating, and entertaining spaces, and a private volume, containing the bedrooms, separated by a two-story glass and steel bridge. A three-story elevator makes the entire house accessible. Despite the many windows, the home is highly energy efficient because of bio-foam insulation, low-e films, and passive solar technologies. There is also has a provision for rainwater collection. Courtesy of Coles Hairston.

Acquavilla

One of the unique features of this Winn Wittman lake-front home are the custom-fabricated cut-aluminum panels that cover the facade and form a decorative screen on many parts of the home. These panels won an award in 2011 as Best New Product from Green Building and Design Magazine. Courtesy of Coles Hairston.

There are thousands of color-changing LED lights spread through the house and the pool, which hangs out over the lake. The ceiling in the living room is covered in silver leaf, and features large white light fixtures designed by Marcel Wanders, which float like fluffy-white clouds. Courtesy of Coles Hairston.

The master suite features a large free-standing tub. This project has been featured on the cover of seven international design magazines. Courtesy of Coles Hairston.

This home is specially designed to fit the fanciful nature of the owner, and to accommodate his large car collection. The garages are more like showrooms, featuring white porcelain floors and specialized lighting. Courtesy of Coles Hairston.

PUBLICATIONS & AWARDS

CARL ABBOTT, FAIA

Abbott, Carl. *IN/FORMED by the LAND*. New York: ORO Editions International, 2013 Monograph on Abbott's Design and Process.
Greer, Diane, Keith Bailey and John Howey. *Florida Architecture: A Celebration*. Washington, DC: American Institute of Architects, 2000, pages: cover, 6, 9, 102, 114, 120-123, 129, 131-132, 137, 163, 167, 172, 182-185.
Boekel, Andrea. *50 Vacation Homes*. Mulgrave, Australia: The Images Publishing Group, 2006, pp. 282-287, 312-319.
Cerwinske, Laura. *Miami Hot & Cool*. New York, NY: Clarkson N. Potter, Inc., 1990, pp. 148-153.
Hasanovic, Aisha. *2000 Architects*. Mulgrave, Australia: The Images Publishing Group, 2006. pp. 133.
Hochstim, Jan. *Florida Modern*. New York, NY: Rizzoli International Publications, 2004. pp. 186-189.
Howey, John. *The Sarasota School of Architecture*. Cambridge, MA: The M.I.T. Press, 1995, pages: cover, 116-118, 158-160, 162-164.
Wagner, Walter F. AIA. *Great Houses*. New York, NY: McGraw-Hill Book Company, 1976, pp. 44-45.
Wagner, Walter F. AIA. *Vacation Houses*. New York, NY: McGraw-Hill Book Company, 1979, p. 174.
Weaving, Andrew. *Sarasota Modern*. New York, NY: Rizzoli International Publications, 2006, pp. 22, 178-189.

AWARDS
1986: College of Fellows, American Institute of Architects
1986: Medal of Honor for Design, Florida / Caribbean AIA
1990: Distinguished Architectural Alumnus Award - University of Florida
1994: Firm of the Year Award, Florida / Caribbean AIA
2000: Millennium Award, Florida / Caribbean AIA
1972 & 2007: Record Houses, Architectural Record
2005, 2007, 2008 & 2010: Test of Time Awards, Florida / Caribbean AIA

ALTERSTUDIO ARCHITECTURE, LLP

"Alterstudio Architects, LlP. An Academic Approach To High-End Design." *Luxury Home Quarterly*, Feb 2011.
"Close Encounters." *Austin Home Magazine*, Fall 2012.
"Return to Elegance." *Entra Magazine*. Nov/Dec 2011.
"This Is It." *Dwell Magazine*, 2011.

AWARDS
2002–2004: Annie Residence
2006: Best Plot In The World Exhibition, Vienna Austria
2007: National German Architecture Museum Exhibition, Frankfurt Germany
2008: National AIA Small Project Design Award
2009: AIA Austin Design Award
2009: Builder's Choice Design Awards
2009: National Dream Home Awards
2010: ACSA Faculty Design Award
2010: AIA Austin Design Awards For Two Residences
2010: Texas Society Of Architects Design Award
2010: The University Of Texas At Austin School Of Architecture Outstanding Scholarship Award
2010: Watermark Design Awards
2011: National Dream Home Awards
2011: Residential Architect Design Award
2012: IIDA Design Excellence Award
2012: AIA Austin Design Award
Texas Society Of Architects Design Award

ANDERSON STUDIO OF ARCHITECTURE AND DESIGN

Catanzarite, Kim. "A Natural Wonder" *Charleston Style & Design Magazine*. Winter 2012.
Harris, Becky. "Tree House Living Inspires Southern Home" Web: February 22, 2013. [http://www.houzz.com/ideabooks/2950857].
Kiawah Island Real Estate. "Designing for Nature: Kiawah Architects Recognized." Web: February 22, 2013. [http://www.kiawahisland.com/blog/view/designing-for-nature-kiawaharchitects-recognized1]

AWARDS
2011: South Carolina AIA Robert Mills Residential Design Honor Awards [http://www.aiascevents.org/SCArchitecture2012/pageflip.html] page 58-65, 72.

BERCY CHEN STUDIO LP

Cullerton, Erin and Michell Galindo. *Young Architects Americas*. Cologne, Germany: Daab, 2009.
Martin, Sam. "Red, wood, and blue." *Dwell*. April/May 2004.
Sirefman, Susanna. *The Contemporary Guest House*. New York, NY: Edizoni Press, 2005.

AWARDS
2005: Urban Reserve
2006: Best Plot In The World Exhibition, Vienna, Austria
2006: Architectural League of New York, Emerging Voices
2007: National German Architecture Museum Exhibition, Frankfurt, Germany

MARLON BLACKWELL ARCHITECT

Arief, Allison, "Mr. Keenan Builds his Tree House," *Dwell*, Aug 2001, pp. 63-67.
Blackwell, M. "A House in the Trees: The Tower House." *OZ Journal*, Volume 25, August 2003.
Broome, Beth. "The L-Stack House bridges city, nature and home." *Architectural Record*, July 2008, pp. 170-173.
Carroll, Diane. "A Creek Runs Through It." *Metropolitan Home*, October 2008, pp. 130-137.
Hyatt, Peter, ed. *Masters of Light: Designing the Luminous House*. Victoria, Australia: The Images Publishing Group, 2007.
Jodidio, Philip, ed. *100 Great Extensions and Renovations*. Victoria, Australia: The Images Publishing Group, 2007.
Phaidon Editors, *Phaidon Atlas of Contemporary World Architecture*. London, England: Phaidon Press Limited, 2009.
Young, Min Woo. "Tower House in Arkansas." *Haute*, Apr 2003, pp. 120-125.

AWARDS
2000-2010: *Dwell* Top 100 Houses We Love
2001: Arkansas AIA Honor Award
2001: Gulf States Regional AIA Honor Award
2005: Arkansas AIA Honor Award
2006: Gulf States Regional AIA Honor Award
2007: Residential Architect Merit Award
2007: Custom Home Merit Award
2007: Arkansas AIA Honor Award
2008: National AIA Housing Award
2008: Custom Home Magazine Merit Award
2008: Gulf States Regional AIA Design Honor Award
2010: Residential Architect Grand Award

CARTON + BURTON ARCHITECTURE P.L.C.

Attmann, Osman. *Green Architecture: Advanced Technologies and Materials*. New York, NY: McGraw Hill. 2010.
"Award winning retreat in Virginia." *World Architecture News*, www.worldarchitecturenews.com, 2007.
"Carter + Burton's Yoga Studio achieves LEED gold certification," *World Architecture News*. www.worldarchitecturenews.com, 2007.
"Enduring Beauty." Green Building and Design blog, *EcoHome Magazine*, July 2012.
Galindo, Michelle. *Masterpieces—Country House Architecture and Design*. Switzerland: Braun Publishing, March 2011.
"Home and Design Portfolio Top 100 Designers." *Home and Design Magazine*, January 2011.
"House of the Month," *Architectural Record Online*, November 2007.
Qu, Anna and Aimee Wu. *Distinctive Residence*. Blaine, WA: Phoenix Publishing, Fall 2011.
Rooney, E. Ashley. *Asian Influenced Architecture*. Atglen, PA: Schiffer Publishing, 2010.
Rooney, E. Ashley. *Shingle Style for the 21st Century*. Atglen, PA: Schiffer Publishing, 2010.
Rooney, E. Ashley. *Shore Design*, Atglen, PA: Schiffer Publishing, 2011.

AWARDS

2000: AIA NOVA, Merit Award, "Matoaka," Clarke County, VA
2005: King Student Medal in Architectural Research
2007: Inform Awards, Excellence in Design (Category Interiors), Honor Award—The Yoga Studio / Guest House
2007: LEED for Homes Gold—The Yoga Studio
2007: The Virginia Society AIA, Jury Citation for Excellence in Architecture—The Yoga Studio / Guest House
2008: 20+10+X Architecture Awards World Architecture Community—The Yoga Studio.
2008: National Capital Region Chapter of the United States Green Building Council, "Small Project of the Year"—The Yoga Studio / Guest House
2008: USGBC "Small Project of the Year"—The Yoga Studio
2008: Inhabitat "Top Ten Green" Award—The Yoga Studio
2008: Northern Virginia AIA Yoga Studio award of Merit
2008: Northern Virginia AIA, Award of Merit in Residential Architecture—The Yoga Studio / Guest House
2012: Northern Virginia AIA Design Awards 2012—Award of Merit in Residential Architecture—Elk Run Ridge

GLAVÈ & HOLMES ARCHITECTURE

Adams, John A. "Seaside Delights, On North Carolina's Outer Banks, Designer Gary Inman Surprises A Homeowner With Rooms Full of Nautical Charm." *Waterfront Home & Design*, 2005.
Belt, Carrie. " French-Country Panache, Natural Materials And Authentic Craftsmanship Call To Mind Le Style Provencal. " *Richmond Times-Dispatch*, 2008.
Lavelle, Lynne. "Poetry In Practice." *Traditional Building*, 2012.
Wamsley, James S. "A Blue Ridge Complex, John W. Kluge's New Additions To His Virginia Estate." *Architectural Digest*, 1997.

AWARDS

2009: Interior Design Excellence Awards: First Place, Hospitality Category
2011: Palladio Award: New Design & Construction Category (More Than 30,000 sf). Sponsor *Traditional Building Magazine*
2012 : Award for Excellence, 2012, Contextual Design Category, Virginia Society AIA
2012: Idea Award: American Society Of Interior Designers & International Interior Designers Association (Virginia Chapter)
2012: Award For Excellence Historic Preservation Category, Virginia Society AIA

FRANK HARMON ARCHITECT PA

"Living The High Life In The Low Country," *Architectural Record*, July 2007.
"Low Country Screens," Residential Architect, May 2006.
Messervy, Julie Moir and Sarah Susanka. *Outside The Not So Big House*. Newtown, CT: Taunton Press. 2006.
"RA 50: the short list of architects we love," *Residential Architect*, December 2010.
"Top Firm: Frank Harmon Architect," *Residential Architect*, 2005.
Trulove, James G. *Tropical Modernism*. New York, NY: Watson-Guptill, 2002.

AWARDS

1993: AIA NC Honor Award—Harmon Residence
1994: AIA Triangle Honor Award—Harmon Residence
1995: AIA SAR (South Atlantic Region) Honor Award—Harmon Residence
2006: Inform magazine Design Awards—Low Country Screens
2006: Residential Architect Design Award, Architectural Details category—Low Country Screens
2007: AIA NC Merit Award—Low Country Residence
2009: AIA National Housing Award—Low Country Residence
2009: Custom Home Magazine Design Awards—Low Country Residence

MCCOLLOUGH ARCHITECTURE, INC.

Morley, Fran. Emerald Coast Home Design, September-October 2004. (Emerald Coast Home Design was redesigned in 2009 to *Coastal Lifestyle Magazine*: their website is www.lifestylemagazine.com).
Van Loon, Benjamin. Interview. *American Builders Quarterly*, January/February/March.

AWARDS

1987: Recipient of the Paul W. Bryant Memorial Scholarship
1988: Jason's Honor Society
1994–1999: Appointed to serve as the Director of the State of Alabama Building Commission
1994–1999: Member of the Governor's Mansion Advisory board; Alabama Historical Commission; and the National Association of State Facility Administrator's Executive Committee
1998: Elected as Southeast Regional President of the National Association of State Facility Administrators
2008: Design Award: Selected as 2008 Master Builder of the year by Star Building Systems

MOON BROS INC. ARCHITECTS

"From Gym to Swim." *Better Homes & Gardens* Special Interest Publication, *Remodel—Ideas Makeovers & Additions*. June/July 2006.
"House & Hostess." *Atlanta Homes & Lifestyles Magazine*, April 2005.
"Magnificent Makeovers." Good Morning America—Dreams Homes, Atlanta, GA.
"The Radar Home." *The Atlantan Magazine*, May/June 2006.
"Rooms with a View." *Atlanta Homes & Lifestyles Magazine*, Aug 2005
"Tree house." *Atlanta Magazine's Home*, Spring 2009.
"Updates for Every Room." *Southern Living Magazine*, May 2005.

SHAWN O'BRIEN INTERIORS

Gambit Cue magazine
http://www.bestofneworleans.com/gambit/charting-a-new-course/Content?oid=1687997.
http://www.bestofneworleans.com/gambit/closet-cases/Content?oid=2024687.
http://issuu.com/gambitneworleans/docs/cue-may2012/19.
http://www.epaperflip.com/aglaia/viewer.aspx?docid=3f1e92a341814883a663e04eeeee2ade.

GUY PETERSON/OFFICE OF ARCHITECTURE

Saxon, Henry. *Four Florida Moderns*. New York, NY: Norton Publishing, December 2009.
Sinovcic, Damir. *50 US Architects*. Culver City, CA: Design Book Press, April 2012, cover & pp. 58-67.
Sinovcic, Damir. *100 Florida Architects & Interior Designers*. Culver City, CA: Design Book Press, 2010, pp. 52-53.

AWARDS
2003: Elected into the College of Fellows of the American Institute of Architects
2007: Lifetime Achievement Award | Sarasota Architectural Foundation
2010: Ivan Smith Endowed Professorship | University of Florida

L. CRAIG ROBERTS, ARCHITECT, AIA

Carabet, Brian G., and John A. Shand. *21st Century Homes: Innovative Designs by North America's Leading Architects*. Piano, TX: Panache Partners, LLC, 2011.
Depiano, Phyllis. "Gracious Comfort." *Victoria*. May/June 2012.
Garlock, Jody. "Vanity Flair." *Better Homes and Gardens*, September 2007.
Martin, Robert. "Great Shower Design Idea." *Southern Living*, February 2010.

THOMAS & DENZINGER ARCHITECTS

Bigner, Melissa. "Natural Instincts." *Charleston Home*, 2011.
Bigner, Melissa. "Right at Home." *Charleston Home*, 2009.
Diedrich, Richard. "Chechessee Creek Club." *The 19th Hole: Architecture of the Golf Clubhouse*. Mulgave, Victoria: Images Publishing Group, 2008.
Konrad, Walecia. "Finally, Kiawah Becomes Trendy (But Don't Touch Those Trees)." *New York Times*, Escapes Section. February 7, 2003.
Lipsky-Karasz, Eliza. "The House That Gucci Built." *The Wall Street Journal Magazine*. 2013.
Morris, Philip. "Nature's Plan." *Southern Accents*, 2003.
Orsini, Tommaso. "Ripartire da un'oasi (To Restart from an Oasis)." *House 24*. Milan, Italy: Il Sole 24 Ore, 2008.
Reasons-Pyles, Katherine. "Natural Beauty." *Huntington Quarterly*, Spring 2011, pp. 52-58

AWARDS
2008: AIA South Carolina Firm of the Year Award.
2012: South Carolina AIA Robert Mills Honor Award

TONIC DESIGN/TONIC CONSTRUCTION

"Houses We Love," Dwell, December 2003.
"Hover Craft," Residential Architect, June 2005.
Trulove, James Grayson. 25 Houses Under 1500 Square Feet. New York, NY: Harper Design, 2004.

AWARDS
2006: AIA North Carolina Honor Award—Chiles Residence
2006: World Architecture News House of the Year—Chiles Residence
2008: Custom Homes Magazine Design Award—Chiles Residence
2008: Metalmag Architecture Award—"Art As Shelter."

ED WEBER ARCHITECTS

Reasons-Pyles, Katharine. "Natural Beauty." *Huntington Quarterly*, Spring 2011, pp. 52-58.

AWARDS
2011: AIA West Virginia Merit Award for Achievement in Architecture in Sustainable Design Private Residence
2011: AIA West Virginia Honor Award for Excellence in Architecture, Haddad Riverfront Park and the Schoenbaum Stage, Charleston, WV
2011: Associated Builders and Contractors, Inc. Excellence in Construction Award New Construction—Residential
2011: Associated Builders and Contractors, Inc. Excellence in Construction Award Historical Restoration/

ANDREW A. WILLETT ARCHITECT PA

Bianchi, Melanie McGee. "Log Cabin Quilt." *Carolina Home + Garden*. Winter, 2011.
Blake, Casey, "Agency Creates 'real home'." *Asheville Citizen Times*, April 21, 2011.
Clark, Paul. "A Touch of Olde England." *Asheville Citizen Times*, November 22, 2008.

WINN WITTMANN ARCHITECTURE

"Acclaim," Luxury Home Quarterly, Winter 2012.

AWARDS
Soaring Wings has won a Dream Home award for Best Contemporary Home of the Year, and was selected as *Architectural Record*'s House of the Month. The project has also been published in the German book *Die Neue Villa*, 2009 and a Chinese book *50 Top Houses*, 2011. The home has also been featured in such magazines as *Robb Report, Spaces* (UK), *HOM* (DL), *Objekt*, (NL) and *Hinge* (HK).
2008: *Architectural Record* - House of the Month
2009: Dream Home Awards: Silver Award winner
2009: *World Architecture News* House of the Year Awards Finalist
2010: Bath of the Year—*Soaring Wings*
2010: Dream Home Awards: Best Innovation in Green Technology

INDEX

Alchemy Designs, 277
Alterstudio Architecture, LLP, 28-29, 300
Anderson Studio of Architecture and Design, 40-54, 300
Andrew A. Willett Architect PA , 268-285, 302
Andrew Crace, 103
Bercy Chen Studio LP, 56-71, 300
C Lighting, 160
Carl Abbott FAIA, 5-10, 18-27, 300
Carter+Burton Architecture, PLC, 84-92, 301
CX Designs, 165
Ed Weber Architects, 252-262, 302
Frank Harmon Architect, PA, 126-137
Gary Inman Home Couture, 95
Glavè & Holmes Architecture, 92-102
Guy Peterson Office of Architecture, 178-184
Guyon Architects / The Studio for Architecture, 104-113
Joe Rankin, 141
Joseph Elko, 95
Julian Chichester, 165
Julie Neill, 167
Karl de Santos, 159
L. Craig Roberts, Architect, AIA, 186-203, 302
Mandala Design, 282
Mark Hampton, FAIA, 114-125
Marlon Blackwell Architect, 71-83, 300
Maxine Snider, 166
McCollough Architecture, Inc., 138-148
McKinnon & Harris, 103
McLean Lighting, 101
Melanie Martin, 148
Moon Bros. Inc. Architects, 150-163, 301
Shawn O'Brien Interiors, 164-177, 302
Sie Matic, 242
Smith Hanes Interiors, 157
Smith Stuart Interiors, 154
Studio Printworks, 172
studioWTA, 204-221
Thomas & Denzinger, 222-243, 302
Tonic Design | Tonic Construction, 235-249, 302
Wallace Architecture, 252-267
William Stewart Designs, 169
Winn Wittman Architecture, 286-299, 302
Yaacov Golan, 160

ACKNOWLEDGMENTS

Each new book is a novel experience, an adventure, and a challenge. There is a reason why we selected these architects for this book. Their work is exciting; they look to the future; and we learn from them.

I was fortunate to have two architects lend their expertise and wisdom to this book. L. Craig Roberts led us on a great exploration of Mobile, Alabama, as we discussed the South today. Carl Abbott drew on his vast experience in making suggestions about areas and people to consult.

BIBLIOGRAPHY

Andrews, Wayne. *Pride of the South.*
New York, NY: New York Athenaeum, 1979.

Foley, Mary Mix. *The American House.*
New York, NY: Harper & Row, 1980.

Hamlin, Talbot. *Greek Revival Architecture in America.*
New York, NY: Dover Publications, 1944.

LaClair, Teresa. *The Southern Colonies: the Search for Wealth (1600–1770).* Broomall, PA: Mason Crest Publishers, 2012.

Rooney, E. Ashley. *Historic Interiors.*
Atglen, PA, Schiffer Publishing, 2011.

Schuler, Stanley. *Mississippi Valley Architecture.*
Atglen, PA, Schiffer Publishing, 1984.

Severens, Kenneth. *Southern Architecture: 350 Years of Distinctive American Buildings.*
New York, NY: E.P. Dutton, 1981.

Thompson, Edgar T. *The Plantation.*
Chicago, IL: University of Chicago, 1932, 2010.

Thompson, Tracy. *The New Mind of the South.*
New York, NY: Simon & Schuster, 2013.

Waterman, Thomas Tileston. *The Mansions of Virginia, 1706–1776.*
Chapel Hill, NC: The University of North Carolina Press, 1945.

Woodward, C. Vann. *Origins of the New South 1877–1913.*
Louisiana State University Press, 1951.